Data Cataloging

Embracing Artificial Intelligence and Machine Learning for Metadata

Jeff Harris

Technics Publications

Published by:

TECHNICS PUBLICATIONS

TECHNOLOGY / LEADERSHIP

115 Linda Vista, Sedona, AZ 86336 USA

https://www.TechnicsPub.com

Edited by Sadie Hoberman

Cover design by Lorena Molinari

First Printing 2023

Copyright © 2023 by Jeff Harris

ISBN, print ed.	9781634622301
ISBN, Kindle ed.	9781634622356
ISBN, ePub ed.	9781634622448
ISBN, PDF ed.	9781634622332

Library of Congress Control Number: 2023940875

Acknowledgments

This is an occasion where I must express my profound gratitude to those close and cherished individuals who played a vital role in the realization of this book.

My family is the core of my existence, and I am intensely passionate about data. Merging these two essential aspects of my life has been challenging, yet the loving family I am fortunate to have has made it a smoother journey. They've supported me at every juncture, even as I penned this book.

To my wife, Elsie, my son, Jean-Michael, and my daughter-in-law, Melissa, I extend my thanks for tolerating the countless hours I spent writing and being my pillar of strength when I needed encouragement. I'm also grateful for the sustenance and frequent offers of assistance that kept me going through my endeavors.

Throughout my career, I've encountered many individuals who have shaped my path and left an indelible mark on my journey. I'm grateful for their influence, which has guided me to this writing project.

Above all, I wish to acknowledge and thank God, who bestowed upon me the wisdom and knowledge necessary to achieve this undertaking. With Him, all things become achievable.

Contents at a Glance

Contents

PART I

Data Cataloging Introduction

CHAPTER 1

Understanding Data Cataloging

What is a data catalog?

In the era of big data and analytics, where we base business decisions on voluminous data sets and insights drawn from them, a critical tool has emerged as an indispensable asset for efficient data management – the "Data Catalog." By creating an organized inventory of a company's data assets and making it easily accessible, a data catalog is a crucial component in any data-driven organization's infrastructure. In this book, we will delve into the concept of a data catalog, its pivotal role, the core components that make it up, and the substantial benefits it offers to businesses. Moreover, we will also discuss the factors to consider while choosing a data catalog that aligns with an organization's unique requirements.

At the fundamental level, a data catalog is a structured and comprehensive inventory of an organization's data assets. It includes an array of assets ranging from databases, tables, files, and reports to analytical models, visualizations, and even algorithms. Each asset provides insightful details, such as its source, nature, usage, and ownership. This body of information is known as metadata and serves as the cornerstone of an effective data catalog.

Data catalogs are not just for a specific type of user; they cater to a diverse audience, including data scientists, data analysts, data stewards, business users, and even decision-makers. Each user group can benefit immensely from the data catalog's capabilities to simplify data discovery, enhance data quality, enable collaboration, and ensure robust data governance.

Integral components of a data catalog

A comprehensive data catalog should feature four key elements:

- **Metadata management.** One of the primary functions of a data catalog is to collect, manage, and organize metadata. This includes a variety of metadata types, such as structural (data types, table names), descriptive (data descriptions, tags), operational (data lineage, creation date), and user-defined metadata. Metadata provides invaluable insights into the properties, context, and potential uses of data assets, helping users understand the potential applications and constraints of the data.

- **Data discovery and search**. The data catalog simplifies the process of discovering and understanding data assets. It should offer robust search capabilities, enabling users to perform keyword-based searches, apply filters, categorize data, and more. These features facilitate rapid identification and comprehension of relevant data, speeding up the data preparation process and enhancing efficiency.

- **Data governance**. Data catalogs are pivotal in enforcing data governance by tracking data lineage, implementing data policies and standards, and ensuring regulatory compliance. They provide functionalities for managing data access, user privileges, and privacy settings, instilling trust in the data and its management.

- **Collaboration tools**. An effective data catalog is more than just a passive repository of data; it is an active platform that encourages collaboration. Features such as annotations, user reviews, ratings, discussion forums, and even data request workflows enable users to share their knowledge, experiences, and needs regarding various data assets, fostering a culture of data collaboration and democratization within the organization.

Factors in choosing a data catalog

Align the selection of a data catalog with your organization's unique needs, scale, and objectives. When choosing a data catalog, certain features need to be considered, such as an intuitive user interface, robust search capabilities, comprehensive metadata management, solid support for data governance, collaboration features, and integration capabilities with existing systems and data sources.

Additionally, the selected data catalog should scale and evolve as per the growth of data in the organization and accommodate changes in data structures and types. The choice between a cloud-based or on-premise solution is another crucial consideration, each having its own benefits and trade-offs.

The evolving role of data catalogs

In today's competitive business landscape, data catalogs have evolved from being a nice-to-have tool to an essential asset in an organization's data management strategy. They play a critical role in the transformation towards a data-driven culture by enhancing data discoverability, improving data literacy, ensuring robust data governance, and fostering collaboration.

Moreover, with data's ever-increasing size and complexity, data catalogs help manage the data deluge and turn it into a valuable resource. They bridge the gap between data and its users, enabling organizations to fully leverage their data assets, thereby driving innovation, efficiency, and growth.

In the final analysis, a data catalog is much more than just an organized inventory of data assets. It's a strategic tool that, when used effectively, can unlock the immense potential of data, empowering organizations to make more informed, accurate, and timely decisions. It paves the way for an organization's journey toward becoming truly data-driven, thereby creating a competitive edge in today's fast-paced data-centric world.

Importance of data cataloging

The advent of the information age has seen the generation of colossal amounts of data unprecedented in human history. This data, sprawling and diverse, harbors within its vast folds, insights capable of transforming the functioning of organizations, economies, societies, and the world at large. Yet, these treasures of knowledge remain inaccessible and inconsequential if not correctly cataloged, indexed, and made navigable.

A data catalog is a structured collection of data used by an organization, described and organized to enable user access. It serves as the yellow pages of an organization's data resources. By cataloging data, organizations can improve decision-making, enhance operational efficiency, comply with regulatory standards, and unlock many business opportunities.

Data cataloging is essential as it bridges the gap between raw data and actionable insights. The vast volume of data organizations generate daily from numerous sources, such as IoT devices, business transactions, customer interactions, and social media posts, often creates a web of complexity that can be nearly impossible to unravel without an effective cataloging strategy.

The task of navigating through the labyrinth of data, identifying relevant information, and leveraging it for actionable insights is eased significantly through a robust data catalog. This catalog enables data scientists, analysts, and decision-makers to find and understand data that is relevant to their work, improving efficiency and productivity.

Moreover, data catalogs provide data lineage, showing where data originates, how it moves through systems, and how it is transformed along the way. This feature is crucial for maintaining data quality, tracking errors, and ensuring regulatory compliance. It also provides greater transparency and fosters trust among data users.

The modern business landscape is characterized by increasing regulatory scrutiny, especially around data handling and privacy, such as Personally Identifiable Information (PII), Protected Health Information (PHI). Regulations such as General Data Protection Regulation (GDPR) and California Consumer Privacy Act (CCPA) mandate organizations to have a clear understanding of their data landscape, including its origin, movement, and storage. Data catalogs aid in compliance by providing a clear view of the organization's data assets, reducing the risk of penalties and reputational damage.

Additionally, the growing prevalence of Artificial Intelligence (AI) and Machine Learning (ML) has emphasized the necessity of having a well-structured, searchable data catalog. It enables these systems to fetch the correct data at the right time, enhancing their effectiveness and precision. It also empowers organizations to have a single version of truth, making it easier for different business units to collaborate and make data-driven decisions.

Despite the many advantages of data cataloging, achieving an efficient and comprehensive data catalog is no small feat. It involves handling a myriad of data formats, integrating data from multiple sources, and continuously updating the catalog as new arrives.

This complex task requires using advanced tools and techniques, including AI and ML, to automate the data cataloging process. Automation not only streamlines the process but also minimizes human errors and enhances data accuracy.

With data cataloging, organizations can establish a clear data governance strategy. Data governance involves the overall management of the availability, integrity, and security of the data employed in an enterprise. A well-structured data catalog forms the backbone of this strategy by providing a clear view of the data landscape and its utilization. Furthermore, organizations can establish clear data ownership, roles, and responsibilities with a catalog in place. It brings clarity, reduces ambiguity, and ensures we treat data as a valuable asset.

With the rise in data democratization, the need for data catalogs has become even more evident. Data democratization refers to the process of making data accessible to everyone in an organization. It empowers individuals to use data in their decision-making processes regardless of their technical expertise.

In a democratized data environment, a well-curated data catalog becomes the Google of organizational data, allowing employees to search for, find, and understand the data they need. It enhances their ability to make data-driven decisions, fostering a data-driven culture within the organization.

Data catalogs not only support internal processes and decision-making. They also play a pivotal role in improving customer experiences. By providing a unified view of customer data, they enable organizations to deliver personalized experiences and targeted marketing campaigns, leading to higher customer satisfaction and increased customer loyalty. Moreover, in an age where data breaches and misuse are frequent, having a data catalog demonstrates a commitment to data privacy and protection, enhancing trust between organizations and their customers.

The future of data cataloging is exciting, with developments such as AI and ML playing an increasingly significant role. These technologies allow for dynamic data cataloging, where catalogs are updated in real-time, making them more responsive and efficient.

Furthermore, these advancements enable predictive cataloging, where the system can anticipate user needs and fetch data even before it is explicitly asked for, ushering in an era of genuinely proactive decision-making.

Despite the immense benefits of data cataloging, it is not a one-size-fits-all solution. Each organization has unique data needs and challenges. The success of a data cataloging endeavor will depend on carefully analyzing these needs and the customization of the cataloging process to meet them.

Moreover, the success of data cataloging is also dependent on people. A culture that understands, appreciates, and respects data is necessary to realize the full potential of a data catalog.

Data cataloging is vital in the modern world, where data reigns supreme. As we step into a future characterized by even greater data generation, the importance of cataloging will only rise. It enables organizations to navigate the vast data oceans, extract relevant insights, make informed decisions, and stay ahead in the fiercely competitive business landscape.

Data cataloging is not just about managing data; it's about unlocking opportunities, powering innovation, and paving the way for a data-driven future.

Benefits and challenges of data cataloging

With businesses relying heavily on data in the digital age, the need for organizing and making sense of this avalanche of information has never been more significant. Data cataloging has emerged as a valuable tool to manage and harness this colossal data, which, if used effectively, can provide substantial competitive advantages, offering critical insights for strategic decision-making and enhancing operational efficiency.

The benefits of data cataloging include:

- **Enhanced data discovery and accessibility.** One of the most critical advantages of data cataloging is the dramatic improvement it brings to data discoverability. Through data cataloging, metadata is organized and indexed efficiently, allowing users to quickly locate the data assets they need, comprehend their context, and use them effectively. This streamlined process minimizes the waste of resources and time traditionally associated with the search and collection of relevant data, thus enhancing the overall productivity of an organization.

- **Improved data quality and consistency.** Data cataloging also plays a pivotal role in augmenting the quality and consistency of data within an organization. When data is cataloged, it becomes easier to visualize the data landscape, enabling organizations to identify issues with data quality. The ability to quickly uncover misclassifications, discrepancies, duplications, and inaccuracies allows for rapid rectification, leading to improved data quality and consistency. High-quality, consistent data forms the bedrock of reliable data analysis and accurate decision-making, both vital in the contemporary business environment.

- **Better data governance and compliance.** A comprehensive data catalog contributes substantially to robust data governance. It keeps an up-to-date and accurate record of all data assets, making it easier to manage and govern data effectively. Furthermore, it simplifies the process of complying with various data laws and regulations. The catalog facilitates tracking and controlling data flow, usage, and security, thereby making adherence to regulatory requirements less cumbersome.

- **Increased user collaboration and data literacy.** Data catalogs often feature collaboration tools that allow users to share insights, document knowledge, and collectively work on data-driven projects. This functionality promotes a culture of data literacy and democratization, empowering every stakeholder in an organization to leverage data for informed decision-making.

Despite its numerous benefits, data cataloging also presents several challenges that need careful navigation. The challenges of data cataloging include:

- **Complexity in data landscape.** In many organizations, data is scattered across diverse platforms and systems, which adds complexity to the cataloging process. Creating a unified and comprehensive data catalog can be daunting, especially when dealing with legacy systems, unstructured data, and different data formats. This complexity increases commensurately with the size of the organization and the diversity of its data sources.

- **Maintaining data catalog.** The dynamism of the data landscape, where new data is continuously generated and existing data is updated or deleted, makes maintaining the data catalog a formidable task. This process requires dedicated resources and sophisticated tools to ensure the catalog is always up-to-date.

- **Security and privacy concerns.** While a data catalog promotes data accessibility, it simultaneously raises concerns about data security and privacy. Implementing appropriate access controls and privacy measures is crucial to ensure that sensitive data is accessible only to authorized personnel.

- **Data catalog adoption.** The practical utility of a data catalog is contingent on its adoption and routine use by the staff. Many organizations grapple with the challenge of encouraging their employees to adopt the data catalog. This requires nurturing a culture of data literacy, providing adequate training, and demonstrating the tangible benefits of using the data catalog.

Strategies for effective data cataloging

Given the benefits and challenges, the key to effective data cataloging lies in strategically addressing these issues:

- **Choose the right tools**. The market offers a wide variety of data cataloging tools, each with its own strengths and weaknesses. The organization's specific needs should guide the choice, the nature of its data landscape, and its technical capabilities. Essential features to consider, include integration with existing systems, automatic cataloging capabilities, scalability, security features, and user-friendly interfaces.

- **Establish clear governance policies**. The data catalog should align with the broader data governance framework of the organization. This includes defining clear data ownership, formulating data usage policies, implementing access controls, and ensuring compliance with relevant data protection regulations.

- **Continuous maintenance and updating.** An outdated data catalog can be more of a liability than an asset. Organizations must prioritize the regular updating and maintenance of the data catalog. Automated data cataloging tools can be particularly useful, as they can keep track of changes in data sources and update the catalog accordingly.

- **Promote data literacy and user adoption.** Fostering a data-driven culture and providing training are crucial to encourage the adoption of the data catalog. We need to make users aware of how the data catalog can make their work more efficient and facilitate better decision-making.

Although data cataloging presents its own set of challenges, its pivotal role in any data-driven organization is undeniable. With an in-depth understanding of the organization's unique needs, careful selection of the appropriate tools, and nurturing a culture of data literacy and collaboration, data cataloging can be a powerful instrument in leveraging the power of data and driving insightful, data-driven decisions. When done right, it's an investment that offers rich dividends in the form of improved business outcomes and enhanced competitiveness.

Key learnings

Data catalogs are indispensable tools for efficient data management in today's data-driven organizations.

A comprehensive data catalog comprises metadata management, data discovery, data governance, and collaboration features.

When selecting a data catalog, consider factors like user interface, search capabilities, metadata management, governance support, collaboration features, and integration capabilities.

Data catalogs have evolved from optional tools to essential assets, enabling data-driven cultures, managing data complexity, and promoting collaboration.

Data cataloging bridges the gap between raw data and actionable insights, facilitating decision-making, operational efficiency, compliance, and business opportunities.

Data cataloging offers enhanced data discoverability, improved data quality, better governance, and increased collaboration, but it also presents challenges related to complexity, maintenance, security, and user adoption.

PART II

Foundations of Data Cataloging

CHAPTER 2

Data Cataloging Principles

Data governance

As we sail further into the Information Age, data becomes the lifeblood of organizations, driving decision-making and strategic planning. With its ever-increasing volume, variety, and velocity, the necessity for proficient data management has escalated, giving rise to modern cataloging and stringent data governance. We will now delve into the intricacies of these two crucial disciplines, exploring their foundations, interconnectedness, and their vital role in shaping an organization's data infrastructure.

Data governance is an integral part of data management, providing a comprehensive framework of policies, procedures, roles, and responsibilities that govern data use, handling, and protection. The principles of data governance include:

- **Data stewardship**. Herein, individuals or groups known as data stewards are assigned to manage the organization's data assets. They ensure that data quality, privacy, and accessibility align with the organization's goals and compliance requirements.

- **Data quality**. This principle insists on maintaining high-quality data that is accurate, complete, timely, and consistent. Tools and methodologies are utilized for data cleaning, validation, and enrichment to ensure data reliability.

- **Data security and privacy**. This relates to securing data against unauthorized access, ensuring confidentiality, integrity, and data availability, and complying with data privacy laws and regulations.

- **Data lifecycle management**. This involves managing data from creation or acquisition through archiving and purging, ensuring effective controls at each stage.

Cataloging, essentially, involves organizing and describing data, similar to how a library catalogs books. This systematic approach ensures quick and precise data retrieval. Data governance is instrumental in guiding cataloging practices to ensure consistency, security, and accuracy through:

- **Data classification**. Data governance sets rules for data classification, facilitating a standardized approach that makes cataloging and retrieval more efficient. We can classify data based on type (structured/unstructured), source (internal/external), sensitivity (public/confidential), or any other relevant factor.

- **Metadata management**. Metadata is data about data, providing context and descriptive details. Data governance helps define standards for creating, updating, storing, and deleting metadata, thus ensuring its accuracy and consistency.

- **Data lifecycle management**. Data governance provides guidelines for managing data throughout its lifecycle – from creation and processing to storage, archival, and disposal. Effective lifecycle management enables efficient cataloging and retrieval, ensuring data is always up-to-date and readily accessible.

Data governance and cataloging are interdependent, each influencing and enhancing the other. Data governance provides the framework for consistency, security, and quality, while cataloging ensures these standards are actualized, enabling quick, easy, and secure data access. We can understand their symbiotic relationship better through the following key points:

- Standardization. Data governance provides the standards for data management, including classification and metadata management.

Cataloging uses these standards to organize and describe data systematically.

- Security. Data governance ensures data security and privacy through policies and protocols. Cataloging respects these rules, managing data securely and providing access only to authorized individuals.

- Quality control. Both contribute to maintaining high data quality. Data governance by establishing quality standards, and cataloging by ensuring data and metadata accuracy through regular updates and validation.

- Regulatory compliance. Data governance sets the course for meeting data-related regulatory requirements. Cataloging is the vehicle that navigates this course, managing data in a compliant manner.

The interplay between data governance and cataloging sets the stage for effective data management. An organization can harness the full potential of its data assets through robust data governance and systematic cataloging. By profoundly understanding these principles and their interconnectedness, organizations can create a strategic data infrastructure that fosters transparency, promotes accountability, ensures security, and drives value from their data.

Data quality and metadata

The rigor of cataloging hinges on the precision and utility of data, rendering the quality of data and metadata indispensable. Let's delve deeper into these concepts, unpacking their complexities.

Cataloging is a fundamental element of library and information science. The accuracy, reliability, and comprehensibility of these catalogs hinge on two interconnected components: data quality and metadata.

Data quality refers to the condition of a set of values of qualitative or quantitative variables that satisfy a set of predefined criteria. While the concept may seem straightforward, it is deeply nuanced in cataloging, with four key dimensions:

- **Accuracy**. The first dimension denotes the extent to which data correctly describes the real-world entity it represents. In cataloging, the data must faithfully represent the attributes of the resource. A minor discrepancy, such as an incorrect author's name or publication date, can result in a misclassification, making the resource challenging to locate or incorrectly identified.

- **Completeness**. The second dimension signifies that all required data about a resource has been recorded. The completeness of catalog data is paramount, as missing data fields can lead to resources being overlooked or misclassified. For example, if a book's ISBN or a journal's ISSN is missing from its record, users may be unable to locate it within a vast collection of resources.

- **Consistency**. The third dimension refers to the uniformity of the recorded data. Consistency in cataloging is crucial in avoiding confusion and enhancing discoverability. For example, we should use the date format consistently across all records. Similarly, author names should be recorded consistently – if a catalog uses an author's full name in one entry, it should not use initials in another.

- **Timeliness**. The fourth dimension considers the currency of the data. Catalogs must be updated as new editions or versions of resources become available. A catalog not reflecting the latest resources could mislead users or render current resources challenging to locate.

These dimensions of data quality are not static or separate entities. They are dynamic and interconnected, with changes in one dimension often affecting the others. For instance, ensuring accuracy might necessitate updates to maintain timeliness, and enhancing completeness might require adjustments to ensure consistency. Regular data quality assessments, such as data auditing and data cleansing, are critical to maintaining these standards and optimizing catalog utility.

Metadata is another essential component of cataloging. It provides structured, detailed information about a resource, which enables effective discovery, retrieval, and management of the resource. We can classify metadata in cataloging into three categories:

- **Descriptive metadata**. This includes data that helps identify and find data assets like names, tags, and descriptions.

- **Structural metadata**. This conveys how complex data assets are put together. It details relationships, formats, models, etc.

- **Administrative metadata**. This provides information to manage and use the data assets, covering aspects like ownership, security, privacy, and usage rights.

Creating metadata involves adhering to established standards that promote uniformity, accuracy, and completeness. Such standards also foster interoperability, allowing different systems to exchange and understand metadata. Common standards in use today include MARC21 (MAchine-Readable Cataloging) for library cataloging, Dublin Core for digital resources, MODS

(Metadata Object Description Schema) for complex resources, and many more.

Achieving high-quality data and robust metadata is a strategic process. It involves careful planning, systematic execution, and ongoing monitoring and adjustment. Here are some critical steps in that process:

- **Crafting a cataloging policy.** A comprehensive cataloging policy should outline the chosen metadata standards and cataloging rules, define the roles of cataloging staff, and reflect the needs of the catalog's user community. This policy acts as a guideline for the cataloging process, ensuring consistency across the board.

- **Investing in staff training.** Regular training in data quality measures, metadata creation, adherence to cataloging rules, and understanding of metadata standards is essential. Well-trained cataloging staff are more likely to produce high-quality records, reducing the need for subsequent corrections.

- **Implementing quality control mechanisms.** Regular audits of cataloging records can identify inaccuracies, inconsistencies, or gaps. This auditing process might involve automated validation tools to check conformance with metadata standards, manual sampling of records for detailed review, and user feedback to identify areas to make improvements.

- **Embracing iterative refinement.** Cataloging is not a one-time task but an ongoing process. We should regularly review and enhance records to improve data quality, accommodate changes in user needs, resource formats, and discovery tools, and reflect new understanding and interpretation of resources.

In essence, high-quality data and well-constructed metadata are foundational to the field of cataloging. Their accurate and thoughtful application is central to the effective organization, discovery, and use of resources. They ensure that a catalog is a robust, precise, and user-centric tool for information retrieval, making it a cornerstone of modern information science.

Data security and privacy considerations

In the vast expanse of the information management universe, cataloging emerges as a discipline of significant importance. In essence, it is the process of creating a structured inventory of resources that provides a systematic approach to accessing and retrieving data. As we move deeper into the digital era, cataloging evolves beyond its traditional library confines, finding new resonance in the realm of digital assets. As data has grown to become the new currency of our modern world, cataloging is more critical than ever. However, the expanding digital universe brings forth a host of challenges, particularly in the realms of data security and privacy. With data breaches becoming increasingly commonplace and a heightened awareness of privacy rights, exploring the intersection of cataloging with data security and privacy considerations is crucial.

Data security

At its core, data security is about implementing measures to prevent unauthorized access to computers, databases, and websites. In the context of cataloging, data security focuses on safeguarding cataloged data against a wide array of potential threats, from human errors to malicious attacks.

Central to data security are the principles of confidentiality, integrity, and availability, often referred to as the CIA triad:

- **Confidentiality.** Confidentiality ensures that access to data is limited strictly to authorized individuals. In cataloging, confidentiality could be maintained by implementing strong access controls and managing permissions meticulously to restrict who can access the data. Encryption, which converts data into a code to prevent unauthorized access, is a potent tool for maintaining confidentiality.

- **Integrity**. Integrity revolves around maintaining the consistency, accuracy, and reliability of data during its entire lifecycle. In cataloging, it implies ensuring that once data is entered into the catalog, it isn't altered or destroyed without authorization. Checksums, cryptographic hashes, and digital signatures are widely used mechanisms to ensure and validate data integrity.

- **Availability**. Availability requires that data should always be accessible when needed. In the context of cataloging, ensuring availability would involve implementing reliable infrastructure, fault tolerance, and disaster recovery plans.

Data privacy

Data privacy, although a related concept, is distinct from data security. It revolves around how data is collected, stored, and shared and the rights of individuals to control their personal information. In the realm of cataloging, privacy considerations emerge due to the potential presence of PII, PHI or other sensitive data within the catalog.

Fundamental principles guide data privacy considerations within cataloging:

- **Data minimization**. The principle of data minimization posits that only the data necessary to fulfill the specific purpose of the catalog should be collected and stored. This approach not only reduces the risk associated with potential data breaches but also respects the privacy rights of individuals.

- **Consent and choice**. Consent is a critical aspect of data privacy. It dictates that individuals must give their informed consent before their data is collected, stored, or used. In cataloging, users should be able to opt out of data collection or withdraw their consent at any point.

- **Anonymization and pseudonymization**. These techniques are invaluable for protecting privacy in a catalog. Anonymization involves removing all identifiable data, making it impossible to trace data back to an individual, while pseudonymization replaces identifiers with pseudonyms, offering an additional layer of privacy protection.

The real power of a data catalog comes from the rich insights we can draw from the collected data. However, with great power comes great responsibility. Balancing data utility and privacy is a critical challenge in cataloging. A host of sophisticated techniques can be applied to strike this balance, including differential privacy and K-Anonymity.

Differential privacy adds a controlled amount of noise to the data, effectively obscuring the contribution of individual data entries. It enables organizations to use and share aggregate data without compromising the privacy of individuals.

K-Anonymity is a privacy principle used to protect the anonymity of individual data within a dataset. It ensures that the data for each individual cannot be distinguished from at least *k-1* other individuals within the dataset. Here's a detailed breakdown:

- **K**. A positive integer that represents the level of anonymity.

- **Equivalence class**. A group of records within the dataset that are indistinguishable from each other based on specific attributes known as quasi-identifiers.

- **Quasi-identifiers**. Attributes or combinations of attributes that could potentially identify an individual, such as age, gender, or postal code.

- **Suppression**. A technique to protect privacy by removing or replacing specific values within quasi-identifiers.

- **Generalization**. A technique to protect privacy by replacing specific values with broader categories within quasi-identifiers.

In a dataset that satisfies k-anonymity, any attempt to link a specific individual to a particular record should result in ambiguity, as there are at least k records that match the individual's quasi-identifiers. This provides a defined level of privacy protection.

This concept is essential for understanding the level of privacy protection that k-anonymity offers. For example, if a dataset satisfies 3-anonymity, then each individual's information is indistinguishable from that of at least two other individuals (i.e., $k-1=2$).

Compliance with data protection regulations is a non-negotiable aspect of cataloging. Different regions have their own specific laws and regulations. For instance, the European Union's GDPR, the CCPA in the US, and Brazil's Lei Geral de Proteção de Dados (LGPD) all lay down stringent rules about how personal data should be handled, stored, and shared.

Emerging trends and future directions

With AI and ML becoming more intertwined with cataloging, new challenges and opportunities arise in terms of data security and privacy. AI algorithms typically require large amounts of data for training, which could lead to potential privacy concerns. Moreover, AI systems can sometimes infer sensitive information even from anonymized data, which presents an entirely new set of privacy challenges.

Techniques like federated learning, secure multi-party computation, and homomorphic encryption help ensure privacy while enabling AI and ML functionalities.

As AI systems become more complex, explaining their decisions becomes crucial, especially when dealing with sensitive data. Incorporating explainability in AI models will be a crucial factor in the evolution of cataloging practices.

Data security and privacy considerations are critical to the foundations of cataloging. Ensuring robust security measures and upholding the privacy of individuals are not just legal necessities but also contribute to the trustworthiness and longevity of the data catalog. Organizations must navigate this complex landscape with a clear focus on upholding user trust, even as they leverage the power of data catalogs to drive insights and innovation.

Key learnings

Data governance is a comprehensive framework encompassing policies, procedures, roles, and responsibilities that oversee data use, handling, and protection. It covers critical aspects like data architecture, integration, quality, security, and privacy.

Data governance establishes rules for data classification, promoting a standardized approach that enhances cataloging and retrieval efficiency.

Data stewardship involves assigning individuals or groups (data stewards) to manage data assets in alignment with organizational goals and compliance requirements.

Data quality focuses on maintaining high-quality data with accuracy, completeness, timeliness, and consistency.

Data security and privacy entail safeguarding data against unauthorized access, ensuring confidentiality, integrity, availability, and compliance with privacy regulations.

CHAPTER 3

Types of Data Catalogs

A data catalog can be viewed as a comprehensive data inventory or a map, enabling users to navigate through the vast data landscape of an organization. This inventory contains metadata, which might include details about the data source, owner, update frequency, underlying tables, definitions, and business context. These catalogs enable easy discovery, understanding, and analysis of relevant data, enhancing accuracy and productivity while reducing the time taken for data-related tasks. Broadly, we can classify data catalogs into four primary types:

- **Traditional data catalogs**. Traditionally, data catalogs were human-curated and managed. They were essentially static lists or repositories that stored metadata about databases and files. Given their manual curation, these catalogs worked efficiently for smaller data volumes but could not scale with the influx of big data.

- **Metadata catalogs**. These catalogs primarily manage metadata. As an evolution of traditional catalogs, metadata catalogs are more dynamic,

providing automatic metadata harvesting. They
trace data lineage and data provenance,
significantly supporting data governance
initiatives.

- **Machine learning data catalogs**. These catalogs
leverage AI and ML capabilities to automate and
streamline data tagging and organization. They
offer recommendations to users based on their data
usage and querying patterns, enhancing the
efficiency of data discovery and use.

- **Enterprise data catalogs**. These catalogs are
comprehensive solutions aimed at managing
colossal data across large organizations. They
combine the features of the other types of catalogs,
including automation, metadata management, and
ML capabilities, with many other advanced
functionalities.

Traditional data catalogs can be visualized as a map for data
professionals, leading them to the required data in the maze
of organizational databases. They are essentially human-
curated repositories that house metadata about the
organization's data assets. Metadata might include details
about the data source, owner, update frequency, related
tables, definitions, and other business-related information.

Traditional data catalogs are usually structured and static,
providing a snapshot of data at a particular point in time.

They are often employed as part of data warehousing or Business Intelligence (BI) systems, assisting users in discovering, understanding, and managing data.

Traditional data catalogs possess several features that are critical for managing and understanding data:

- **Metadata management**. Traditional data catalogs provide a repository for metadata. This metadata can be descriptive (e.g., data definitions, ownership details), structural (e.g., table schemas, relationships), or administrative (e.g., creation dates, access controls).

- **Data lineage**. While not universally true, some traditional data catalogs can track data lineage, showing the life cycle of a data asset from its source to its current state.

- **Searchability**. Traditional data catalogs provide the ability to search for data assets. While not as advanced as the search features in more modern data catalogs, this functionality helps users locate needed data assets within the catalog.

- **User access controls**. Traditional catalogs often include the ability to set user access controls, ensuring that sensitive data is only available to authorized personnel.

Even though they may lack the sophisticated automation and ML capabilities of their more modern counterparts, traditional data catalogs provide several benefits:

- **Improved data discovery**. By centralizing metadata, traditional data catalogs make it easier for users to discover and locate the necessary data.

- **Better data understanding**. Traditional data catalogs help users understand the context and meaning of data, including its source, how it's been transformed, and who owns it.

- **Support for data governance**. Traditional data catalogs can be an essential tool for data governance, helping organizations track their data assets and how they're used.

Despite their benefits, traditional data catalogs have several limitations:

- **Lack of scalability**. Traditional data catalogs often struggle to handle the scale of today's big data environments. The manual curation process cannot efficiently keep up with the pace of data creation and change in modern organizations.

- **Limited search and query capabilities**. Compared to modern data catalogs, traditional catalogs' search and query capabilities can be limited. This

can make it harder for users to find the data they
need, especially in large data environments.

- **No AI/ML capabilities**. Unlike their modern
  counterparts, traditional data catalogs do not offer
  AI/ML capabilities. This means they cannot
  automate tasks like data classification, data quality
  profiling, or provide user recommendations.

- **Dependency on human intervention**. Due to the
  absence of automation, maintaining traditional
  data catalogs can be labor-intensive, requiring
  manual updates whenever there are changes to
  data assets.

Evolution of traditional data catalogs

As organizations have grappled with ever-increasing
volumes of data, the limitations of traditional data catalogs
have become more pronounced. This has led to the
evolution of more sophisticated types of data catalogs,
including metadata catalogs, ML data catalogs, and
enterprise data catalogs.

These modern data catalogs offer numerous enhancements
over traditional catalogs, such as automation, ML
capabilities, improved search features, and more robust
integration with other data management tools and

platforms. However, many of these improvements build on the foundations laid by traditional data catalogs, including the centralization of metadata and the provision of a standard interface for data discovery and understanding.

Despite their limitations in today's big data environments, traditional data catalogs have played a crucial role in the evolution of data management. Their contribution to centralizing metadata, facilitating data discovery and understanding, and supporting data governance efforts have been significant.

While modern organizations might find more value in the automation and advanced capabilities offered by newer types of data catalogs, understanding the strengths and weaknesses of traditional data catalogs provides valuable context. This knowledge can inform decisions about the implementation of data management tools and strategies and help organizations appreciate the journey that data management has taken from the era of traditional data catalogs to the sophisticated enterprise data catalogs of today.

Deep dive into metadata catalogs

In a world inundated with data, data catalogs serve as an indispensable tool for organizations to navigate, understand, and exploit their vast and diverse data assets effectively. Among the various types of data catalogs, Metadata Catalogs have emerged as a significant evolutionary step beyond Traditional Data Catalogs. This section focuses on Metadata Catalogs, exploring their key features, benefits, drawbacks, and applications.

Metadata Catalogs are repositories that store and manage metadata. Metadata provides contextual information about data assets, including details such as the data source, owner, definition, lineage, relationships, quality indicators, and more.

As an evolution of Traditional Data Catalogs, Metadata Catalogs bring more dynamic capabilities, incorporating automatic metadata harvesting and sophisticated metadata management features. They are crucial tools for data governance, enabling organizations to maintain data consistency, quality, and security.

Metadata Catalogs carry a suite of features that extend beyond those offered by Traditional Data Catalogs:

Automated metadata harvesting. Metadata Catalogs automatically gather metadata from various data sources, reducing manual curation efforts and improving accuracy.

- **Data lineage and provenance**. These catalogs provide insight into the life cycle of data assets, tracking their source, transformations, and how they have been used over time. This is particularly beneficial for data auditing and maintaining data integrity.

- **Sophisticated metadata management**. Metadata Catalogs support advanced management of metadata, allowing users to view, edit, and organize metadata in ways that align with their specific business context and requirements.

- **Integration capabilities**. Metadata Catalogs can often integrate with a variety of data management tools and platforms, making it easier to maintain a coherent and updated view of the organization's data landscape.

- **Search and query capabilities**. While not as advanced as ML or Enterprise Data Catalogs, Metadata Catalogs often have improved search capabilities compared to Traditional Data Catalogs, allowing users to locate necessary data assets more efficiently.

- **Security and compliance**. By providing an overview of the organization's data and usage, Metadata Catalogs can support security and compliance efforts, helping enforce access controls and compliance with data privacy regulations.

Metadata Catalogs bring a range of benefits to organizations:

- **Efficient data discovery**. By centralizing metadata, Metadata Catalogs make it easier for users to discover and understand the data they need, boosting productivity and accelerating data-driven decision-making.

- **Improved data governance**. Metadata Catalogs provide crucial capabilities for robust data governance. They help maintain data consistency, track data lineage and provenance, ensure data quality, and comply with regulatory standards.

- **Increased data accessibility**. Through improved search and query capabilities, Metadata Catalogs increase the accessibility of data, making it easier for both technical and non-technical users to leverage data assets.

- **Support for data security and compliance**. Metadata Catalogs can significantly support data security and compliance efforts by offering a clear view of data assets, along with their usage and lineage.

Despite their numerous benefits, implementing Metadata Catalogs also comes with challenges:

- **Complexity of integration**. Given the diversity of data sources and tools in an organization, integrating a Metadata Catalog with all of them can be complex and time-consuming.

- **Maintaining data quality**. Ensuring that the metadata within the catalog is accurate, up-to-date, and consistent is an ongoing challenge that requires continuous effort.

- **Lack of advanced features**. While Metadata Catalogs offer more advanced features than Traditional Data Catalogs, they may still lack some of the capabilities provided by Machine Learning Data Catalogs or Enterprise Data Catalogs, such as AI-driven data classification, tagging, and recommendation features.

While Metadata Catalogs offer a significant advancement over Traditional Data Catalogs, the ever-increasing scale and complexity of data environments necessitated the development of more sophisticated types of data catalogs. Machine Learning Data Catalogs and Enterprise Data Catalogs represent the next steps in this evolutionary trajectory, offering enhanced automation, AI/ML capabilities, more advanced search features, and more comprehensive data governance features.

Understanding the strengths and weaknesses of Metadata Catalogs can inform decisions about implementing data management strategies and selecting the correct type of data catalog to meet an organization's unique needs.

Deep dive into machine learning data catalogs

As the digital universe continues to expand, organizations need practical tools to manage, understand, and utilize their diverse data assets. An essential step in this process is the use of data catalogs. A pivotal advancement in this area has been the emergence of Machine Learning Data Catalogs.

Machine Learning Data Catalogs are a leap forward from Metadata Catalogs, employing AI and ML techniques to automate and enhance data cataloging processes. They represent the integration of data cataloging with AI and ML, driving automated metadata generation, data classification, and recommendation capabilities.

Machine Learning Data Catalogs take the metadata management capabilities of traditional catalogs a step further with automated systems that can learn from user interactions, understand patterns, and make intelligent recommendations.

Machine Learning Data Catalogs come equipped with a range of advanced features:

- **Automated metadata generation.** Machine Learning Data Catalogs automate the process of metadata collection and generation. They can extract metadata from various data sources and automatically classify and tag data.

- **Data classification and tagging.** Leveraging AI and ML, these catalogs can automatically classify data and add tags based on predefined rules and learned patterns, simplifying data discovery and management.

- **Intelligent search.** Machine Learning Data Catalogs often come with advanced search features, including semantic search and Natural Language Processing (NLP) capabilities, making it easier for users to find the data they need.

- **User interaction analysis and recommendations.** These catalogs can learn user patterns and preferences by analyzing user interactions, providing personalized data recommendations, and enhancing user productivity.

- **Data lineage and provenance.** Similar to Metadata Catalogs, Machine Learning Data Catalogs can track data lineage, showing the life cycle of a data asset from its source to its current state.

- **Integration capabilities.** These catalogs often offer robust integration capabilities with various data sources and tools, ensuring that the catalog stays up-to-date with the latest changes in the data landscape.

Machine Learning Data Catalogs bring substantial benefits to organizations:

- **Streamlined data discovery**. With automated metadata generation, data classification, and intelligent search features, these catalogs significantly simplify the data discovery process.

- **Improved user productivity**. Machine Learning Data Catalogs can enhance user productivity and drive better decision-making by learning from user interactions and making personalized data recommendations.

- **Enhanced data governance**. These catalogs can support robust data governance efforts by providing detailed data lineage, automated tagging, and classification.

- **Accelerated time to insight**. With their advanced features, Machine Learning Data Catalogs can accelerate the process of deriving insights from data, helping organizations become more agile and responsive.

Despite their myriad benefits, Machine Learning Data Catalogs also pose some challenges:

- **Algorithmic transparency and bias**. As with any AI/ML system, there can be issues of algorithmic transparency and bias. Users need to understand how the system makes recommendations, and measures must be in place to ensure that the system does not reinforce or perpetuate existing biases.

- **Implementation complexity.** Implementing a Machine Learning Data Catalog can be complex, requiring significant technical expertise. Organizations must also consider data privacy and security concerns when using these catalogs.

- **Maintaining data quality.** While these catalogs automate many aspects of data management, ensuring the accuracy and quality of the data and metadata within the catalog remains a crucial task that requires ongoing effort.

The next evolutionary step from Machine Learning Data Catalogs is the development of Enterprise Data Catalogs. These catalogs offer all the benefits of Machine Learning Data Catalogs and more, providing a unified, holistic view of the organization's data landscape. They include advanced features like data privacy management, workflow integration, collaboration tools, and enterprise-level scalability.

Machine Learning Data Catalogs represent a significant advancement in the realm of data cataloging. They offer substantial benefits in terms of data discovery, user productivity, data governance, and time to insight. Despite some challenges in implementation and maintenance, they have become essential tools for data-driven organizations.

Deep dive into enterprise data catalogs

Enterprise Data Catalogs emerge as powerful tools for large corporations dealing with voluminous and diverse data across varied sources. They utilize AI and ML to automate data cataloging, data classification, and data management, reducing manual labor and increasing accuracy and efficiency across the enterprise.

Enterprise Data Catalogs offer a rich palette of features to ensure robust data management:

- **Automated data discovery**. Enterprise Data Catalogs can automatically discover data across various sources, reducing the need for manual intervention and keeping the catalog updated with minimal effort.

- **Advanced metadata management**. Enterprise Data Catalogs offer extensive metadata management capabilities. This includes automatic metadata harvesting, lineage tracking, version control, and the ability to annotate metadata with additional attributes.

- **Machine learning and artificial intelligence.**
  Enterprise Data Catalogs apply ML and AI
  algorithms to automate various processes,
  including data classification, tagging, and profiling.
  These technologies enable personalized
  recommendations for users based on usage
  patterns and predictive analytics for the potential
  use of data assets.

- **Data governance.** Enterprise Data Catalogs
  provide robust data governance capabilities. They
  track data lineage, data provenance, and data usage
  to ensure compliance with data regulations and
  standards. They help enforce data access controls
  and privacy policies.

- **Collaborative and social features.** Enterprise Data
  Catalogs often incorporate collaboration tools
  allowing users to share data, collaborate on
  analysis, and rate or review data assets. These tools
  promote a data-driven culture and foster trust in
  data.

- **Search and query capabilities.** Enterprise Data
  Catalogs provide powerful search and query
  capabilities, including semantic search, filtering,
  and faceted search, making data discovery faster
  and more precise.

- **Integration capabilities.** Designed to work in harmony with various data management tools and platforms, Enterprise Data Catalogs can integrate with data integration tools, BI tools, data lakes, and data warehouses, ensuring smooth data workflows.

- **Security and compliance.** Enterprise Data Catalogs offer stringent security measures, including data masking and encryption, to safeguard sensitive information. They also help in enforcing compliance with various data privacy regulations.

The implementation of Enterprise Data Catalogs brings a host of benefits:

- **Improved data discovery and understanding.** Enterprise Data Catalogs centralize metadata and provide powerful search capabilities, making data discovery and understanding simpler and faster.

- **Increased data trust and quality.** Features like data lineage, version control, and user reviews increase trust in data and improve data quality.

- **Enhanced compliance and governance.** Robust data governance capabilities provided by Enterprise Data Catalogs help organizations comply with regulatory standards and improve data privacy and security.

- **Increased efficiency and productivity.** Automation of data cataloging and personalized recommendations increase efficiency and productivity.

- **Collaborative environment.** Collaboration features in Enterprise Data Catalogs foster a data-driven culture and encourage cross-functional collaboration, leading to more informed decision-making.

- **Cost efficiency.** Enterprise Data Catalogs can save significant costs by reducing manual labor and speeding up data discovery and analysis.

Despite their numerous advantages, implementing Enterprise Data Catalogs isn't without its challenges:

- **Integration complexity.** Integrating an Enterprise Data Catalog with all of a large organization's broad range of data sources and tools can be complex and time-consuming.

- **Data privacy and security.** Ensuring data privacy and security, especially when dealing with sensitive data, can be challenging. Access controls and privacy policies need to be meticulously managed.

- **User adoption.** Like any new technology, user adoption can be a challenge. Comprehensive training and change management initiatives may be required to ensure users can effectively utilize the Enterprise Data Catalog.

- **Maintaining data quality**. While Enterprise Data Catalogs can enhance data quality, maintaining high-quality data in the catalog is an ongoing task that requires continual effort and vigilance.

- **Scalability**. As data volumes continue to grow, ensuring the Enterprise Data Catalog scales to accommodate this growth can be a significant challenge.

Enterprise Data Catalogs offer an effective solution to the challenges of managing and understanding data in large organizations. They amalgamate various features that can significantly enhance data discovery, understanding, governance, and collaboration. While the implementation of an Enterprise Data Catalog can pose particular challenges, the benefits it offers in data management, regulatory compliance, productivity enhancement, and cost savings far outweigh these. However, successful implementation requires careful planning, stakeholder buy-in, effective training, and ongoing maintenance.

Key learnings

Data catalogs are classified into four primary types: Traditional Data Catalogs, Metadata Catalogs, Machine Learning Data Catalogs, and Enterprise Data Catalogs.

Traditional Data Catalogs are manually curated repositories that store metadata about data assets, providing structured and static information.

Metadata Catalogs automate metadata harvesting, support data lineage and provenance, and offer advanced metadata management features.

Machine Learning Data Catalogs use AI and ML to automate data cataloging processes, improve data classification, and offer intelligent search and recommendations.

Enterprise Data Catalogs are comprehensive solutions that automate data discovery, enhance metadata management, and integrate with various data sources and tools.

CHAPTER 4

Data Cataloging Architecture

Data has emerged as the most critical resource in today's digital era, driving businesses, scientific research, and even our everyday interactions. However, the sheer volume, variety, and velocity of data, compounded by the need for compliance with increasingly stringent regulations, have made data management a complex challenge. To overcome these issues, organizations have turned to data catalogs. This section will provide an in-depth understanding of data cataloging architecture, delving into the core components of a data cataloging system and how they interact.

The data cataloging architecture is the holistic model that defines how different components related to data cataloging are organized, interacted, and performed. It involves these five layers:

- **Data source layer.** Includes all the different sources from where data is generated or gathered, such as databases, data warehouses, file systems, APIs, and other data storage units.

- **Data ingestion layer**. Fetches the data from different sources, cleans and pre-processes it, and ensures its availability for further cataloging.

- **Data cataloging layer**. Houses the actual data catalog, which organizes and catalogs the ingested data.

- **User interface layer**. Provides an interface for users to access, explore, and manage the data catalog.

- **Security and Governance Layer**. Governs access controls, permissions, and privacy constraints.

Components of a data cataloging system

Data source layer

Data sources are the places where data resides. In modern organizations, data sources are usually diverse and distributed, including databases, data warehouses, data lakes, APIs, files, external data feeds, and even social media feeds. These sources can be structured, semi-structured, or unstructured and exist in on-premises servers, cloud platforms, or hybrid environments.

Data ingestion layer

Metadata extractors connect to the data sources, identify relevant data, and extract metadata from them. Metadata includes technical metadata (data type, size, creation date, etc.), operational metadata (data lineage, data quality metrics, etc.), and business metadata (data definitions, data owner, business context, etc.).

Metadata extractors can take various forms depending on the type of data source. They can be database connectors for databases, APIs for web services, or crawlers for unstructured data. They must be robust, flexible, and able to handle various data types, formats, and connectivity protocols.

Data cataloging layer

The data cataloging layer is broken down into two parts, the data catalog engine and the metadata database.

The data catalog engine is the heart of a data catalog. It processes and organizes metadata stored in the metadata database, building a structured and searchable catalog. The engine employs a variety of techniques, such as data classification, semantic discovery, relationship inference, and ML, to enhance the usability of the catalog.

Data classification categorizes data into predefined classes. Semantic discovery identifies the meaning of data entities and attributes based on their names, descriptions, and contexts. Relationship inference identifies relationships between data entities based on usage, common attributes, and other clues. ML can automate these tasks and improve their accuracy over time.

The metadata database is where all extracted metadata is stored. This database needs to be highly scalable to accommodate the growing volume of metadata, especially in large organizations with numerous data sources. It must also provide strong support for queries and data modeling to enable easy retrieval and understanding of metadata.

User interface layer

The data catalog user interface is the front end through which users interact with the catalog. It must be intuitive and user-friendly, enabling users to search, explore, understand, and use the cataloged data efficiently. The UI often includes features such as a search bar, data lineage visualizer, data dictionary, data profiling reports, and collaboration tools for users to annotate and discuss data.

Security and governance layer

The security and governance layer is a critical component that ensures the data catalog complies with data security policies, privacy regulations, and governance frameworks.

It manages user access control, data privacy, audit logging, and policy enforcement.

Access control involves authenticating users and authorizing them to access specific data based on their roles. Data privacy involves masking or anonymizing sensitive data to prevent unauthorized access. Audit logging records all actions taken in the catalog for future review. Policy enforcement checks that all data handling practices comply with the organization's data governance policies.

Interaction between the components

The components, as mentioned earlier, do not work in isolation; instead, they interact in an orchestrated manner to provide a seamless data cataloging experience. The metadata extractors continuously extract metadata from the data sources and feed it into the metadata database. The data catalog engine then processes and organizes this metadata, updating the catalog. Users can access and interact with this catalog through the user interface. All these interactions are governed by the security and governance layer, ensuring compliance with regulations and policies.

A well-architected data catalog is an integrated system where changes in one component ripple through the other components. For example, if we add a new data source, the metadata extractor connects to it, extracts metadata, and sends it to the database. The catalog engine processes this new metadata, and the catalog is updated. Users can then see and interact with this new data through the UI.

Data catalogs are essential in modern data-driven organizations, empowering users to discover, understand, and use data assets efficiently. To deliver these benefits, a data catalog needs a robust architecture composed of several interconnected components, including data sources, metadata extractors, a metadata database, a data catalog engine, a user interface, and a security and governance layer.

By understanding these components and their interactions, organizations can better design, implement, and manage their data catalogs, ensuring they maximize the value of their data assets and comply with regulatory requirements. As data continues to grow in volume, variety, and importance, the role of well-architected data catalogs will only become more critical.

Metadata management

Metadata describes the actual data and offers insights into its content, context, and structure. It's a high-level overview that helps users find relevant data and understand its potential value. Hence, managing this metadata is crucial for effective data cataloging.

Metadata management involves the administration and organization of metadata to ensure its accuracy, integrity, and usability. It includes functions like metadata ingestion, metadata storage, metadata search, and metadata governance. Each of these functions forms a pillar that supports the effective cataloging and utilization of data.

Metadata ingestion

Metadata ingestion involves extracting metadata from various data sources. The primary challenge in metadata ingestion is the diversity in data sources and the metadata they produce. These sources can vary from relational databases, NoSQL databases, APIs, data lakes, and data warehouses. Each of them can have different types of metadata associated with them, such as structural metadata, descriptive metadata, administrative metadata, and reference metadata.

To address this, the data cataloging architecture should have a robust metadata ingestion mechanism that can handle heterogeneity and scale. This requires a flexible, modular approach that can adapt to various data sources and metadata types.

The mechanism should also be capable of extracting both technical metadata (e.g., data type, column name) and business metadata (e.g., business definitions, data lineage). While technical metadata is often straightforward to extract, business metadata may require advanced techniques like NLP and ML to extract meaningful information from business documents, data dictionaries, and other sources.

Metadata storage

After ingesting the metadata, it needs to be stored in an organized manner to facilitate easy discovery and access. The challenge here is to structure the metadata storage in a way that caters to different types of metadata while ensuring scalability and performance.

Typically, metadata is stored in a metadata repository, which can be a relational database, a NoSQL database, or a graph database, depending on the requirements. For instance, a graph database can be particularly beneficial for storing metadata as it can intuitively represent complex relationships between different metadata entities.

To ensure efficient retrieval, metadata should be appropriately indexed. It might also be beneficial to store metadata in a denormalized format for quick querying even though it might consume more space.

Metadata search

An effective search mechanism is vital for making helpful metadata. Users should be able to find relevant metadata quickly, which can be challenging given the volume and complexity of metadata.

The search functionality should support not just keyword-based search, but also semantic search to understand the context and return more relevant results. It should also support advanced search features like faceted search, which allows users to narrow down the results by applying multiple filters.

AI and ML can play a significant role in enhancing search capabilities. For instance, ML algorithms can rank search results based on their relevance, and NLP can be employed to better understand user queries.

Metadata governance

Metadata governance involves defining and enforcing policies related to metadata management. It ensures that metadata is accurate, consistent, secure, and complies with the relevant regulations.

Metadata governance includes these four components:

- **Metadata standardization**. This involves defining standards for metadata to ensure consistency. It can include naming conventions, data types, formats, and other rules.

- **Metadata validation**. It checks the accuracy of metadata and verifies that it adheres to the defined standards.

- **Metadata privacy**. This deals with the privacy aspects of metadata. It ensures that sensitive information is not exposed through metadata and complies with privacy regulations like GDPR and CCPA.

- **Metadata auditing**. It tracks the changes made to metadata over time for accountability and traceability.

In essence, metadata governance is about putting suitable checks and balances in place to maintain the integrity and value of metadata.

The power of metadata management

Metadata management is a critical part of the data cataloging architecture. Organizations can enhance their data discovery, data understanding, and data governance capabilities by efficiently ingesting, storing, searching, and governing metadata.

A robust metadata management architecture can empower users to find the correct data at the right time, understand its context and value, and use it confidently while complying with the necessary rules and regulations. It can turn the data catalog from a passive repository into a dynamic, intelligent platform that accelerates data-driven decision-making and innovation.

In a nutshell, metadata management is not just about managing metadata but about leveraging it to unlock the true potential of data. As we continue to generate and accumulate more data, the importance of metadata management in data cataloging architecture will only increase. Therefore, it's time to pay attention to metadata management and invest in building a robust, scalable, and intelligent metadata management architecture.

Integrating data sources

As data volumes explode, businesses and organizations increasingly face the challenge of managing and utilizing disparate data sources. In this context, data catalogs are pivotal in empowering stakeholders to efficiently find, understand, and use these resources. Integrating data sources into a data cataloging architecture involves identifying, preparing, and merging data from various sources into a centralized system for easy access and analysis. This integration involves several steps, including identifying data sources, preparing data, data ingestion, metadata management, and data governance.

Identifying data sources

The first step in integrating data sources into a data cataloging architecture is identifying what data is available and its location. Businesses usually have data stored in a variety of forms, such as relational databases, NoSQL databases, flat files, data lakes, data warehouses, and even in cloud-based systems. It's critical to perform a comprehensive audit of these data sources, considering their relevance and quality for the intended use. This step involves business and technical teams working together to identify relevant data and ensure its quality.

Preparing data

Once we identify data sources, the next step is to prepare data for integration. This process can involve cleaning data, handling missing or inconsistent data, resolving schema conflicts, converting data into a suitable format, and ensuring data security. The goal is to ensure the data is reliable, accurate, and secure before it is ingested into the catalog. Data preparation is usually performed using ETL (Extract, Transform, and Load) tools or data preparation tools designed to handle large volumes of data from various sources.

Data ingestion

The next stage is data ingestion, which refers to the process of importing, transferring, loading, and processing data for later use or storage in a database. It's essential to consider both batch and real-time data ingestion capabilities, depending on the requirements of the business. During ingestion, metadata is also captured, which plays a crucial role in data cataloging. It provides context and additional information about the data, like data lineage, data source, data format, and data update frequency. This metadata helps to make the data more discoverable, understandable, and usable in a data catalog.

Metadata management

Metadata management is a crucial aspect of a data cataloging architecture. It involves the organization, integration, and control of metadata across the organization to ensure data consistency, integrity, and usability. This includes managing technical metadata (like data types and data length), business metadata (like business rules and data ownership), and operational metadata (like data lineage and data profiling). The data cataloging solution's metadata management tools or capabilities can capture, store, manage, and search metadata.

Data governance

The final and ongoing step in integrating data sources into a data cataloging architecture is data governance. It involves setting policies, standards, and processes to ensure data is used and managed appropriately, securely, and effectively. This includes establishing data privacy and security measures, data quality checks, data access controls, data usage policies, etc. Data governance ensures that data in the catalog is trusted, secure, and compliant with regulations.

Integrating data sources into a data cataloging architecture is a complex but necessary process for businesses dealing with large volumes of disparate data. It involves multiple steps, from identifying data sources to implementing data governance. The goal is making data easily accessible, understandable, and usable for stakeholders. With a proper data cataloging architecture in place, organizations can maximize the value they derive from their data.

Scalability and performance considerations

In the realm of big data, where data sources are diverse and the data volume is vast, efficient data cataloging becomes crucial. As data continues to grow both in variety and volume, it becomes necessary to design a data cataloging architecture that is not only scalable and performs efficiently but is also capable of handling the increasingly complex requirements of data management.

Scalability is a crucial attribute of any system that aims to grow and handle an increasing amount of work. In the context of data cataloging, scalability refers to the ability of a system to handle an increasing amount of data, users, and queries without a significant drop in performance. Data cataloging systems must be designed with scalability in mind from the start, as data volumes and data complexity are only going to increase with time.

A scalable data cataloging system should be able to:

- **Handle an increasing amount of data**. With the rise of big data, organizations can accumulate terabytes or even petabytes of data. The system should be capable of ingesting, cataloging, and managing this amount of data efficiently.

- **Support a growing number of users**. As more people within the organization start using the data catalog, the system should be able to handle an increasing number of concurrent users.

- **Process a growing number of queries**. Users interact with the data catalog by issuing queries. The system should be capable of handling and processing an increasing number of queries concurrently.

- **Performance considerations in data cataloging.**
  Performance is another critical attribute of a data
  cataloging system. The system should not only be
  capable of handling a large volume of data but
  should also do so efficiently. We measure the
  efficiency in terms of the system's response time
  and throughput.

Several performance considerations should be taken into
account when designing a data cataloging system:

- **Query processing speed.** This is the time it takes
  for the system to process a query and return the
  results. This is one of the most critical performance
  indicators, as it directly impacts the user
  experience.

- **Indexing speed.** The speed at which new data can
  be ingested and cataloged by the system. We
  should quickly and efficiently catalog each data
  source after adding it.

- **Metadata extraction and management.** The speed
  at which the system can extract, catalog, and
  manage metadata from various data sources. This
  includes both structured metadata (such as data
  type, column name, etc.) and unstructured
  metadata (such as data descriptions, annotations,
  etc.).

A scalable and high-performing data cataloging architecture should incorporate several fundamental design principles:

- **Distributed computing.** Distributing the data and the computational workload across multiple nodes can significantly improve both scalability and performance. This approach allows the system to handle more data and process queries more quickly.

- **Data partitioning.** This involves dividing the data into smaller, manageable chunks (partitions) that can be processed in parallel. This not only improves performance but also allows the system to scale horizontally by adding more nodes.

- **Indexing.** This is a crucial component of any data cataloging system. Indexing improves the query processing speed by allowing the system to locate the required data quickly. The choice of indexing method (bitmap indexing, B-tree indexing, hash indexing, etc.) can significantly impact performance.

- **Caching.** Storing frequently accessed data in a cache can significantly improve performance by reducing the need to access the underlying storage system.

Distributing the workload evenly across the nodes in the system can prevent any single node from becoming a bottleneck and thus improve overall performance. In addition to the above design principles, there are several advanced techniques that can further enhance the scalability and performance of a data cataloging system:

- **Data compression.** Compressing data can reduce the required storage space and improve data transfer speed. However, compression can also increase CPU usage, as we need to decompress the data before processing it.

- **Query optimization.** Optimizing the way queries are processed can significantly improve performance. This could involve techniques such as query rewriting, query caching, and using cost-based query optimizers.

- **Using in-memory databases.** Storing data in memory (as opposed to disk) can dramatically improve performance. However, this approach can be more expensive and may not be suitable for all types of data.

- **Using a columnar storage format.** Unlike row-based storage, which is optimized for transactional data, columnar storage is optimized for analytical workloads and can significantly improve the performance of analytical queries.

Designing a scalable and high-performing data cataloging architecture involves carefully considering various factors, including the volume and complexity of the data, the number of users, the types of queries, and the hardware and software resources available. By adopting appropriate design principles and advanced techniques, it is possible to build a data cataloging system that can effectively manage the growing data needs of modern organizations.

Key learnings

A thorough understanding of data cataloging architecture, encompassing data source, ingestion, cataloging, security, and user interface layers, is pivotal for effectively managing and utilizing data in modern organizations.

Components within a data cataloging system are interdependent and interact in a coordinated manner to provide a unified data cataloging experience, necessitating the integration of these layers to optimize the functionality of the data cataloging architecture.

A meticulously constructed data catalog enhances user ability to efficiently discover, comprehend, and utilize data assets, playing a vital role in optimizing data-driven decision-making processes within an organization.

Understanding the components of a data catalog and their interactions enables organizations to proficiently design, implement, and manage their data catalogs, ensuring maximization of data assets value while complying with applicable regulations and requirements.

PART III

Building an Effective Data Catalog

CHAPTER 5

Data Profiling and Data Discovery

Data profiling is a vital aspect of building an efficient data catalog. It refers to the systematic analysis and understanding of the nature and quality of the data stored in a database or a data source. This initial phase of the data management process is crucial to ensuring the usability and reliability of data over time.

At a high level, data profiling consists of gathering statistics or informative summaries about data to identify potential areas of improvement in terms of data quality, integrity, consistency, and security. The ultimate goal is to provide comprehensive knowledge about the data that is useful in various data-intensive tasks such as data integration, data transformation, or data model refinement.

Data profiling techniques can range from examining the statistical summary of data to identifying outliers, dependencies, and anomalies. These can offer insights into aspects such as data format, data distribution, value ranges, uniqueness, and missing values.

Importance of data profiling

Data profiling plays an essential role in effectively creating and maintaining a data catalog. It is the step where we explore the nature of data and identify the potential issues. The insights generated from this process are valuable for:

- **Data understanding.** Data profiling allows data scientists and other data professionals to gain a comprehensive understanding of their data. It helps them know the characteristics, limitations, and potential of the data, aiding in better decision-making.

- **Data quality assurance.** Through the process of data profiling, one can identify and address data quality issues such as missing or incorrect data, discrepancies, and inconsistencies, thereby enhancing data quality.

- **Data governance.** Data profiling enables organizations to ensure data governance. It helps define and implement rules, roles, and responsibilities related to data management. Data profiling ensures that all data in a catalog follow specific standards and policies, ensuring consistency and reducing risks.

- **Data integration.** By understanding the nature and structure of data, organizations can make better decisions about data integration. It supports the process of combining data from different sources into a unified view, which is crucial for many business applications, including analytics, BI, and ML.

Profiling techniques and steps

Building a comprehensive and accurate data catalog involves different data profiling techniques and steps, including:

- **Data collection.** The first step involves gathering data from various sources. This involves identifying and accessing data from different sources such as databases, data lakes, cloud storage, and more. Appropriate methods for data extraction are chosen depending on the type of data and the source.

- **Data assessment.** Once the data is collected, it is evaluated for completeness, accuracy, and relevance. This involves statistical analysis and visualization to understand the data's distribution, variability, and other essential characteristics. The data is evaluated based on predefined quality parameters such as completeness, uniqueness, timeliness, validity, consistency, and accuracy.

- **Metadata extraction**. Metadata provides information about other data, making retrieving, using, and managing data easier. Metadata extraction involves extracting and storing information such as the data source, data type, creation time, modifications, and more.

- **Anomaly detection**. Anomaly detection is an essential aspect of data profiling that involves identifying unusual, suspicious, or anomalous data points that deviate from the norm. These anomalies can be due to various reasons, such as data entry errors, measurement errors, or even indicative of a particular event or issue.

- **Pattern recognition**. Identifying patterns in data helps understand data behavior and predict future trends. Pattern recognition can include finding recurring patterns, identifying associations and correlations, and discovering sequences.

- **Dependency identification**. Identifying dependencies among the data attributes helps understand the relationships and associations among different data elements. It helps in understanding the data structure, redundancies, and opportunities for normalization.

- **Reporting and visualization**. The last step involves summarizing and visualizing the data profiling results. This can involve creating data dictionaries, reports, charts, or dashboards that provide an overview of the data's health and quality.

Profiling tools

Various data profiling tools in the market can automate the profiling process, making it faster, more accurate, and more efficient. These tools can perform tasks, such as data collection, metadata extraction, data assessment, anomaly detection, and more. Some popular data profiling tools include Informatica Data Explorer, IBM InfoSphere Information Analyzer, Oracle Enterprise Data Quality, and Talend Data Quality.

In conclusion, data profiling is a critical step in building an effective data catalog. It provides insights into the quality, structure, and semantics of the data, enabling organizations to make informed decisions and effectively manage their data assets. Through a systematic data profiling process, organizations can enhance their data's usability, reliability, and value, enabling them to drive better decision-making, improve operations, and gain a competitive edge.

The techniques and steps in data profiling provide a foundation upon which we can build a robust data catalog. By understanding and implementing these techniques, data professionals can build an effective data catalog that serves as a valuable resource for their organization.

The key to an effective data catalog lies in the understanding that data is a dynamic and evolving asset. As such, the process of data profiling is not a one-time activity but a continuous process of discovery, assessment, monitoring, and refinement to keep the data catalog up-to-date and relevant.

Building an effective data catalog is not an end in itself, but a means to an end – a step towards becoming a data-driven organization. Thus, data profiling should be seen as an ongoing strategic activity, integral to an organization's data management strategy.

Data discovery techniques

Data discovery is an integral part of constructing an efficient data catalog. It involves exploring data from different sources, understanding its semantic meaning, and making it easily searchable and accessible to data consumers. This process is not only crucial in identifying what data resides within an organization but also in determining its relevance and usability. Without effective data discovery, any data catalog is at risk of becoming a digital landfill.

Automated data discovery

Automated data discovery uses advanced algorithms and ML to scan through databases and other data repositories, automatically identifying and categorizing data. It's much faster than manual data discovery, making it an ideal choice for organizations with large, complex data ecosystems.

Automated data discovery tools can extract metadata from a variety of sources, including databases, cloud storage, business applications, and even unstructured data repositories. They can recognize common data elements, like names and addresses, and can often categorize data by type (personal data, financial data, etc.).

These tools also play an essential role in data governance by helping organizations comply with regulations like GDPR and CCPA. By identifying sensitive data, organizations can better manage and protect it, reducing the risk of data breaches and non-compliance penalties.

Semantic data discovery

Semantic data discovery is another technique that leverages metadata and ontologies (a structured framework for organizing and interpreting data) to understand and describe the context and meaning of data.

Semantic data discovery uses the concepts of entities and relationships. Entities represent data objects, such as a customer or a product, and relationships describe how entities are connected. For instance, a customer can have a relationship with a product through a purchase.

Semantic discovery can help find the underlying relationships between different data items and enable a more profound understanding of the data, which cannot be easily done with conventional discovery methods. It can uncover patterns and dependencies in the data that are not immediately apparent, thus providing valuable insights for decision-making.

Manual data discovery

Despite the advances in automated and semantic discovery techniques, there's still a place for manual data discovery in the data cataloging process. This method involves human users reviewing and tagging data manually.

Manual data discovery allows for personalized input and nuanced understanding that automated tools may not capture. For instance, data experts within the organization can add context to data by noting specific use cases or business rules associated with particular data elements.

However, this technique is time-consuming and may not be practical for large datasets. It's typically used in conjunction with automated data discovery, with the automated tools doing the initial heavy lifting and human experts fine-tuning the results.

Data discovery best practices

- **Understand your data landscape**. Before beginning data discovery, it's essential to have a comprehensive understanding of your organization's data landscape. This includes knowing your data, its location, and who has access to it.

- **Leverage artificial intelligence and machine learning**. These technologies can significantly speed up the data discovery process and provide more accurate results than manual methods. They can also help identify patterns and relationships in your data that might otherwise go unnoticed.

- **Establish a data governance framework**. Data discovery is most effective when it's part of a broader data governance strategy. This framework should include policies and procedures for data access, usage, and security, as well as roles and responsibilities for data management.

- **Enable collaboration**. Data discovery should be a collaborative process involving both technical and business users. This can help ensure the data catalog is relevant and valuable for everyone in the organization.

- **Iterative approach**. Data discovery is not a one-time event but an ongoing process. As we add new data sources and existing ones change, you must regularly update your data catalog to ensure it remains accurate and current.

Effective data discovery techniques are critical in building an effective data catalog. By leveraging automated, semantic, and manual discovery methods, organizations can create a comprehensive, accurate, and usable data catalog that supports their data governance goals and enhances decision-making capabilities.

Using metadata for data profiling

In a data-driven business landscape, the ability to effectively organize, understand, and analyze data is essential. One tool fundamental to achieving these objectives is a data catalog – a structured and organized inventory of data assets that aid in their discoverability and usability. The key to unlocking the true potential of a data catalog lies in the effective utilization of metadata.

Metadata provides vital information about the content, context, quality, and structure of data, akin to a detailed library catalog card for a book.

Metadata's importance is multi-fold. It helps in data discovery, understanding data relationships, assessing data quality, and facilitating proper data governance.

Metadata can be classified into descriptive, structural, and administrative categories.

Descriptive metadata

Descriptive metadata typically encompasses data that helps in finding and working with specific instances of data, including information about a resource's content and context. This type of metadata may include free-form text, controlled vocabularies, unique identifiers such as DOI (Digital Object Identifier), and elements like title, author, abstract, keywords, and classification codes.

Cataloging, archiving, discovering, and identifying resources heavily rely on descriptive metadata, and standardized vocabularies and controlled languages (e.g., Library of Congress Subject Headings – LCSH, Medical Subject Headings – MeSH) are often employed to improve precision and recall in information retrieval. Organizations must establish standard practices around its generation, validation, and maintenance to manage and govern this metadata efficiently.

Controlled vocabularies should be agreed upon and adopted across the organization to eliminate ambiguity and inconsistency. Taxonomies and ontologies can further be employed to form logical groupings and infer semantic relationships between data entities.

Structural metadata

Structural metadata emphasizes the organization and relationship within data, providing insights into how components of data entities interrelate, are ordered, and form cohesive units. This understanding is vital for digital objects like XML documents, e-books, or complex files that may include images, transcripts, and audio files. Structural metadata describes how these elements are bound together and how pages, chapters, or sections are interrelated, enabling users to navigate complex resources more effectively.

Effective governance of structural metadata ensures that the organization and relationship of data components are consistently represented. Rules around the definition and articulation of such metadata should be put in place, and the structure should be intuitive to accommodate the complexity and diversity of the data resources within the organization. Standardized schemas such as METS

(Metadata Encoding and Transmission Standard) are commonly used to convey this information, reinforcing the uniformity and accessibility of structural metadata.

Administrative metadata

Administrative metadata is integral to the management, use, preservation, and insights into resource usage of data resources. It encompasses several subtypes, each serving a specific purpose:

- **Rights management metadata.** Defines and controls access levels to data resources, including licensing information, copyrights, and other legal data. Clearly defining this aspect is crucial for enforcing appropriate access, thereby protecting sensitive information and intellectual property rights.

- **Preservation metadata.** Maintains and archives data for the long term, preservation metadata includes the history of data modifications, migration information, and other activities essential for digital preservation. With the rise of digitization and regulatory requirements, robust strategies for preserving data are vital.

- **Technical metadata.** Speaks to the technical aspects of the data resources, such as file types, formats, sizes, creation, and modification details. Proper documentation of technical metadata ensures data usability and system interoperability.

Collectively, administrative metadata supports the resource's management and is critical for maintaining digital rights, ensuring long-term digital preservation, and offering insights into how resources are used. The well-structured and detailed nature of administrative metadata plays a foundational role in the governance of data within an organization.

Best practices for defining metadata types

Defining metadata types should be a meticulous and well-planned process. Here are details on the best practices:

- **Standardization**. Adopting standardized formats for metadata, such as Dublin Core or ISO 19115 for geographic information, ensures consistency and enables easier data sharing and collaboration between different systems or organizations.

- **Collaboration**. Collaboration between data producers, curators, and consumers is crucial in understanding the varying perspectives and requirements for metadata. Each stakeholder provides unique insights into how metadata should be defined and utilized.

- **Training**. Training helps stakeholders understand the importance and intricacies of metadata. This awareness promotes consistency and accuracy in metadata creation and utilization. Training sessions can be conducted in person or through digital platforms, and they should be regularly updated to cover any changes in tools or procedures.

- **Automation**. Metadata creation can be a tedious and error-prone process if done manually. Where applicable, automating metadata creation and updating with the help of AI and ML technologies can significantly improve efficiency and accuracy.

- **Regular reviews**. As the data and business needs evolve, so too should the metadata. Regular reviews of metadata definitions ensure that they remain relevant and valuable. These reviews can also uncover any inconsistencies or errors that may have crept in.

- **Metadata type registry**. A metadata type registry serves as a central repository for all metadata type definitions. It should be easily accessible to stakeholders and should clearly document each metadata element, its meaning, usage instructions, and any other relevant information.

A clear understanding and effective management of different metadata types are instrumental in harnessing the full potential of an organization's data. By implementing these best practices, organizations can ensure that their metadata is accurate, consistent, and valuable for various data operations.

Data profiling involves examining the data available in an existing database and collecting statistics and information about that data. The goal of data profiling is to gain a better understanding of the quality of data and to uncover data anomalies.

Data profiling aids in identifying inconsistencies, anomalies, and redundancies in data, facilitating data cleansing and enhancing the reliability of data-driven insights.

Metadata provides critical context to data and aids in understanding data structures, data types, relationships, and data quality, thereby playing an instrumental role in data profiling. Metadata can help understand data at a granular level, decipher patterns and relationships among data sets, and assess the overall quality and reliability of the data.

Metadata can indicate potential areas of concern, such as missing values, inconsistency in data values, outdated information, and lack of data standardization. These are the red flags that data profiling seeks to uncover and address.

Steps in leveraging metadata for data profiling

Leveraging metadata for data profiling involves several steps:

- **Metadata collection.** Using tools and techniques to collect metadata from different data sources. The process might involve automated collection using APIs, manual collection for legacy systems, and even web scraping for external data sources. The challenges lie in dealing with heterogeneous data sources, varying data formats, and volumes of data.

- **Metadata management.** Once collected, metadata must be effectively stored, organized, and managed. A metadata repository is an essential part of this process, enabling centralized metadata storage and access. Metadata must be kept up-to-date, consistent, and standardized across the organization.

- **Metadata analysis.** This process gleans insights from metadata to understand the underlying data better. Tools and techniques used in metadata analysis vary from simple descriptive statistics to complex ML models.

- **Implementing metadata in data profiling.** Applying the results of metadata analysis in data profiling improves data understanding and management. It involves integrating insights gained from metadata analysis into the data profiling process to enhance data quality, reliability, and usability.

For example, a multinational corporation might have diverse data sources across various regions. By using metadata for data profiling, the company can understand data structures, relationships, and quality across all its sources. It can uncover data inconsistencies, redundancies, and anomalies, ultimately leading to improved data governance, compliance, and data-driven decision-making.

Best practices in using metadata for data profiling

Some of the best practices when using metadata for data profiling include:

- Regularly updating and maintaining the metadata repository to reflect the changes in the underlying data.

- Ensuring that metadata standards are implemented and adhered to across the organization.

- Using automated tools for metadata collection, management, and analysis wherever possible.

- Integrating metadata management with data governance and data management policies.

The future of metadata in data profiling

Looking forward, ML and AI promise to automate many tasks in metadata management and data profiling. For instance, ML algorithms can automatically generate and update metadata, identify patterns in metadata, and detect data quality issues. Blockchain technology can offer immutable, secure metadata management, ensuring the reliability and authenticity of metadata. As data volume and complexity increase, metadata's role in data profiling will only become more significant and crucial in the future.

Key learnings

Data profiling, a vital facet for curating an efficient data catalog, serves as the foundational stage of the data management process, establishing the underpinnings for sustainable data usability and reliability throughout its lifecycle.

Executed at a broad level, data profiling encapsulates the collection of data statistics or summaries aimed at spotlighting possible areas for enhancement across data quality, integrity, consistency, and security.

The overarching aim of data profiling pivots towards furnishing exhaustive knowledge about the data, becoming an invaluable asset in various data-centric activities, such as data integration, transformation, or model refinement.

Employed techniques in data profiling may span from scrutinizing the statistical summaries of data to pinpointing outliers, dependencies, and anomalies, thereby enabling a broad-spectrum analysis of data properties.

By leveraging these techniques, valuable insights into aspects like data format, distribution, value ranges, uniqueness, and the prevalence of missing values can be derived, thereby enhancing the overall management and utility of the data catalog.

CHAPTER 6

Data Cataloging Best Practices

Data standardization

Data standardization is essentially the method of modifying data to fit a standard format. It's the bedrock of data integration, enabling fluid interoperability and ensuring uniformity in diverse datasets. Standardization is a necessary prerequisite to any data-driven process, ensuring a single version of the truth and facilitating efficient data analysis.

Refining data formats for consistency

Consistency is paramount in data standardization. When dealing with vast amounts of data collected from multiple sources, a lack of consistency can lead to significant issues. It's essential to establish a comprehensive data dictionary or a set of standard data definitions that provide guidelines for data entry. This dictionary should define the acceptable formats for each data field. Moreover, a combination of automated checks and manual oversight can be implemented to ensure consistent adherence to the established formats. This proactive approach to maintaining consistency not only makes data processing more straightforward but also improves data reliability and trustworthiness.

Adapting to evolving standard protocols

While adopting standard protocols forms the backbone of effective data standardization, it's crucial to stay updated with the evolving landscape of these standards. As technology advances and industries evolve, data standards also undergo transformations. Thus, a continuous learning approach is essential to align with the most relevant and updated protocols.

Maintaining an active presence in relevant professional bodies and staying updated with the latest industry literature can help organizations stay ahead of the curve in adapting to evolving standard protocols.

Automated standardization tools and AI

Automated standardization tools have evolved significantly, with many now leveraging AI and ML for advanced functionalities. These tools can learn from existing data patterns and apply those learnings to new data, significantly improving the efficiency of the standardization process.

These tools offer features like anomaly detection, data transformation, and automatic correction of data inconsistencies. The use of AI and ML in data standardization also extends to understanding context and semantic standardization, thereby enhancing the overall quality of data standardization.

Data categorization

Data categorization, the methodical classification of data into meaningful, defined categories, is a powerful tool in data governance. It boosts data discoverability and accessibility, making it essential for any successful data strategy.

Complex hierarchical structuring

Hierarchical data categorization is more than just a top-down categorization approach; it's about creating logical, intuitive, and user-friendly data categories. A well-thought-out hierarchical structure would reflect the organization's business structure and processes.

In more complex cases, multiple hierarchical structures may be created to cater to different user needs. This approach, known as polyhierarchy, allows a single data entity to exist in multiple categories, depending on the context of use.

Metadata management in categorization

Metadata plays a pivotal role in effective data categorization. However, managing metadata, especially for large organizations, can be a complex task. Adopting a robust metadata management strategy is crucial for maximizing the benefits of metadata in data categorization.

The strategy should include the identification of critical metadata elements, standardization of metadata, and the establishment of a metadata repository. Implementing a metadata management tool can further streamline this process, facilitating the automated collection, storage, and maintenance of metadata.

Periodic reviews and agile categorization updates

As businesses evolve, the data they generate and collect also changes. To keep the categorization schema relevant and effective, periodic reviews and agile updates are vital. This involves not just adding new categories but also decommissioning old ones that no longer serve any purpose.

An agile approach to data categorization ensures that the data catalog remains responsive to business changes. This involves adopting a feedback mechanism where users can suggest changes or improvements to the categorization schema. Data standardization and categorization are vital for effective data cataloging. As data volumes and variety continue to grow, organizations must evolve their standardization and categorization practices to maintain a high-quality user-friendly data catalog.

Creating an effective data schema

Understanding the business context

Before creating your data schema, invest time in understanding the nuances of the business processes, current and future requirements, and how data impacts these aspects. Analyze the business functions and determine the types of data necessary for their operations. This should also take into account any regulatory requirements and anticipated changes in business strategy or technology. Review existing data systems to identify gaps, redundancies, and opportunities for integration. Gathering this information is essential to build a data schema that caters to the current and evolving needs of the business.

Modeling data according to requirements

After gathering the necessary insights about the business, you can start designing your data schema. This involves identifying entities, their attributes, and their relationships. An entity could be any object in the business that needs to be tracked, such as customers, products, orders, etc. Attributes are properties or characteristics of these entities, and relationships define how different entities interact with each other.

Entity-Relationship Modeling can be a valuable tool in this process, helping visually represent the data structure and facilitating better understanding and communication among stakeholders. Additionally, choosing appropriate data types is crucial to maintain data integrity, optimize storage, and improve query performance.

Entity-Relationship Modeling is a popular method to represent the data model, which includes entities (tables), attributes (fields), and relationships (links between tables). This technique facilitates better communication among stakeholders, thus making the data schema more understandable and effective.

When creating fields within your tables, be mindful of the type of data that each field will hold. Appropriate data types not only prevent incorrect data entries but also optimize storage and improve query performance.

Keys and indexes play a critical role in establishing relationships between data and enhancing data retrieval speed. Primary keys ensure each record in a table is unique and identify each piece of data in a table. Foreign keys link records across different tables, enabling data relationships. Indexes, used to speed up the retrieval of data, can significantly enhance query performance. However, it's important to exercise restraint when creating keys. Over-indexing can lead to performance issues due to the additional overhead during data updates.

Both normalization and denormalization manage data redundancy and read performance. Normalization involves organizing a database into tables and columns to minimize data redundancy and improve data integrity. It can be beneficial in transactional systems where data integrity is paramount. Denormalization involves combining tables to improve read performance at the cost of some data redundancy. It can be beneficial in analytical systems where query speed is more important than data storage.

Data integrity is about ensuring the accuracy, consistency, and reliability of data in the database. We can implement different types of integrity constraints. Domain integrity involves defining the valid set of values for a column using data types, unique constraints, check constraints, and NOT NULL constraints. Referential integrity ensures that relationships between tables remain valid. It is typically enforced using foreign keys.

Schema documentation

Thorough documentation of your data schema is crucial to ensure it can be easily understood and maintained over time. Document each table, field, data type, index, relationship, and any business rules or constraints. This information should be kept updated and easily accessible to all relevant stakeholders.

Periodic review and update

The data schema is not a one-time task. It needs to be revisited and revised as the business evolves. Regularly review your schema to ensure it is still aligned with the current business needs and take into account any changes in technology or regulatory requirements.

Leveraging data catalog tools

Data catalog tools can automate many aspects of schema creation, from data discovery and classification to governance. They provide a single, unified view of your data assets across various sources, making it easier for users to understand and use data effectively. Data catalog tools also support collaboration with features that allow users to annotate and share data insights. By using these tools, organizations can ensure a more efficient and streamlined approach to data management.

Creating an effective data schema is a comprehensive task that requires understanding the business context, modeling the data, implementing keys and indexes, applying normalization and denormalization, imposing data integrity rules, documenting, and reviewing and updating the schema. By following these best practices, businesses can better manage their data, gain valuable insights, and make more informed decisions.

Tagging and taxonomy design

In the world of data, chaos is the natural state. Data, in its raw form, is akin to crude oil, unstructured and unwieldy. Extracting value from it requires refinement, and one of the critical steps in this process is data cataloging. This involves collecting metadata about the raw data, storing it systematically, and making it searchable. In this context, the art of tagging and taxonomy design becomes paramount.

Tagging

Tagging plays an indispensable role in enhancing data discoverability and usability. Tagging, in its simplest definition, is the process of assigning metadata to datasets, serving as a means to describe, categorize, and identify data in an efficient, easy-to-understand manner.

Tags are pivotal in ensuring smooth data navigation, boosting data governance, and enhancing data security. This section delves into the nuances of designing an effective tagging system, elucidating the importance of clarity, consistency, extensibility, automation, and verification.

Clarity and consistency

Tagging begins with creating a clear and consistent set of labels that can be easily understood and employed by all stakeholders in the organization. The effectiveness of a tagging system hinges on its clarity and consistency.

In terms of clarify, every tag should provide a straightforward, intuitive insight into the data it represents. Avoid using obscure acronyms, industry jargon, or overly technical terms unless they are widely recognized and understood across the organization. The idea is to make the tags comprehensible to both technical and non-technical users.

Consistency in tagging facilitates uniformity and avoids confusion. For instance, if you tag some datasets related to customer information as "customer data" and others as "client data," it can lead to potential confusion. It's crucial to have a standardized tagging protocol to maintain uniformity.

Extensibility

As the data landscape of an organization evolves, the tagging system must adapt to accommodate new data sources, data types, and business requirements. This necessitates designing a tagging system that is extensible.

An extensible tagging system is flexible and can accommodate the addition, modification, or removal of tags as required without disrupting the existing system. When developing a tagging system, anticipate potential future changes and growth in the organization's data environment and business needs.

Automation

Manually tagging vast amounts of data can be an arduous and error-prone process. Given the volume, velocity, and variety of data in today's digital organizations, automating the tagging process becomes imperative. Leverage ML and NLP technologies to automate the tagging process as much as possible. Automated tagging not only reduces the time and effort involved but also enhances the accuracy of the tagging system.

Verification

Tags, though automated, require regular verification to ensure their accuracy and relevance. Incorrect or outdated tags can lead to misinterpretation of data and potential issues with data governance.

Implement a system of regular audits to check the correctness and relevance of tags. This could involve manual checks, automated data validation tools, or a combination of both. Regular verification helps maintain the reliability of the tagging system and enhances data integrity.

Tagging is a cornerstone of effective data cataloging. A robust tagging system can significantly enhance data discoverability and usability, driving efficient data-driven decision-making processes. Despite the seeming simplicity, creating a well-designed tagging system demands careful planning, consistent governance, and a continuous improvement mindset.

The value of a well-executed tagging system extends beyond just organization and classification; it forms the backbone of efficient data discovery, accessibility, security, and governance. Therefore, regular reviews and updates to your tagging system are essential to ensure it continues to serve its purpose and deliver its potential value effectively.

Taxonomy design

If tagging lays the groundwork for data organization, taxonomy design builds the structure. A well-designed taxonomy system based on tags, organizes data into systematic hierarchies or categories, making navigation and governance more efficient.

In its essence, taxonomy design involves the classification of data into specific, defined categories based on certain characteristics or features, often represented by tags. Doing so brings order to the vast, often chaotic, data landscape, facilitating improved access, insight, and governance. This section delves deeper into designing a robust and effective taxonomy system.

The primary objective of a taxonomy is to make sense of data from a business perspective. The taxonomy should reflect the business's structure, workflows, objectives, and users. We should design the taxonomy to accommodate the needs of the end-users, typically business stakeholders who rely on the data for decision-making, analysis, and strategic planning. When designing the taxonomy, start with the broader business areas and then drill down into more specific categories. This hierarchical approach aligns with the typical structure of business operations, thus making the taxonomy more intuitive and easy to use for business users.

Effective taxonomy design hinges on the principle of hierarchy. The top-level categories could represent broad data domains, such as Sales, Marketing, HR, or Finance, with sub-categories representing more specific data subsets within these domains.

The hierarchical design brings multiple benefits:

- **Ease of navigation**. Users can quickly drill down from general categories to specific ones, making data discovery faster and more efficient.

- **Improved governance**. Hierarchies facilitate better data governance by allowing clear assignment of ownership and accountability at each level.

- **Efficient search**. Hierarchical taxonomy improves search functionality by narrowing down the search scope at each level.

Standardization is a critical aspect of taxonomy design. Similar to tagging, the terms used in taxonomy should adhere to standard conventions understood across the organization or even across the industry.

Following a standard nomenclature ensures that the taxonomy system can be easily understood and used by all stakeholders, including those who may not be deeply involved in data management. It also ensures that your taxonomy can easily integrate with other systems or databases, enhancing interoperability and flexibility.

Taxonomy design is not a one-time process. As the business evolves, its data requirements also change. Regular reviews of the taxonomy system are necessary to ensure that it continues to serve the changing needs of the organization effectively.

Use feedback from users and data analytics to identify areas for improvement. Continuous improvement and iteration help maintain the relevance and effectiveness of the taxonomy system.

Taxonomy design, built upon a robust tagging system, is vital to unlocking the potential of your data. By organizing data into a systematic, hierarchical structure that reflects business operations, taxonomy design significantly enhances data accessibility, usability, and governance.

However, designing and maintaining an effective taxonomy system requires careful planning, regular review, and iterative improvements. Keeping your taxonomy system aligned with your business structure and needs ensures that your data remains a valuable, accessible, and manageable asset, driving informed decision-making and strategic insights.

Designing a clear, consistent, and extensible tagging system

The first step in creating an effective data catalog is designing a robust tagging system. Here are some best practices:

- **Clarity and consistency.** The tags used should be easily understood by all stakeholders. Acronyms or industry jargon should be avoided unless they are well-known across the organization. The same information should be consistently tagged in the same way across datasets. Consistency also extends to the level of granularity – avoid mixing highly specific tags with broad, generic ones.

- **Extensibility**. Data evolves, and so should your tagging system – plan for growth and changes in data sources and types. Make sure the tagging system is flexible enough to adapt without requiring massive rework.

- **Automation**. Manual tagging is time-consuming and error-prone. Leverage ML and NLP technologies to automate tagging as much as possible.

- **Verification**. We should regularly verify tags to ensure accuracy. Implement a system of regular audits, potentially utilizing automated data validation tools.

Establishing a taxonomy design

Once you have a tagging system in place, the next step is to design a taxonomy based on these tags. A few important guidelines are:

- **Business-centric**. The taxonomy should reflect the business' structure and requirements. It's not about what makes sense to the data scientist but about what makes sense to the business user.

- **Hierarchical**. Taxonomies are most effective when they are hierarchical. Top-level categories could represent broad data domains (e.g., Sales, HR, Finance), while sub-categories represent more specific data subsets.

- **Standardization**. Just as with tagging, the taxonomy design should adhere to industry or internal standards to ensure cross-system compatibility and user comprehension.

Bridging tagging and taxonomy through governance

Finally, both tagging and taxonomy systems require robust data governance policies. Without them, both systems risk devolving into disorder. Governance should enforce consistency, audit compliance, and facilitate continuous improvement. It should also involve the relevant stakeholders from different parts of the business to ensure that the catalog remains aligned with business needs.

Tagging and taxonomy design are critical to effective data cataloging. When done correctly, they enable faster, more efficient data discovery and use, driving better business decision-making. Designing and implementing these systems is a non-trivial task, requiring careful planning, consistent governance, and the involvement of multiple stakeholders. However, the effort pays dividends in the form of a more data-driven, efficient, and effective organization.

A data catalog is a living entity. It should evolve with your data and your business needs. Therefore, regularly review your tagging and taxonomy systems to ensure they remain relevant and practical. By doing so, you lay the foundation for a truly data-driven organization.

Leveraging AI and ML

As the volume and variety of data continue to surge in the digital era, managing this data effectively has become a significant challenge for organizations. One promising solution to this challenge is the data catalog. Data catalogs enable users to effectively discover, understand, and utilize data assets by providing a centralized inventory of data sources. Traditional data cataloging practices can be manual, time-consuming, and prone to human error. Leveraging AI and ML can automate this process, increase accuracy, and derive more value from data assets.

Automated data discovery and classification

Automating data discovery and classification has several steps. It begins with data ingestion, bringing data from various sources into the system. We can use AI algorithms to identify and connect to these different data sources.

In the discovery phase, AI-powered crawlers explore these sources, identifying data and extracting metadata. AI can analyze data contents, recognize patterns, and classify data accordingly. For instance, ML algorithms can identify patterns in how specific data is used and predict that similar data is likely to be used in the same way, thereby aiding in classification. AI can also apply semantic recognition to understand and classify data based on its meaning and context. This dramatically enhances the catalog's ability to categorize data accurately.

Metadata management

Metadata management involves creating, maintaining, and using metadata. AI and ML can significantly enhance this process. For instance, AI can be used to generate descriptive metadata such as titles, tags, and summaries, enhancing the catalog's searchability and usability.

Furthermore, AI algorithms can create relational metadata, which specifies relationships between data assets. This is useful for understanding data lineage and dependencies.

ML can identify patterns in how data assets relate to each other and predict future relationships. In addition, ML algorithms can analyze metadata for insights. For instance, anomaly detection algorithms can identify inconsistencies or abnormalities in metadata, indicating potential data quality issues or security vulnerabilities.

Data quality assessment

Data quality refers to the accuracy, consistency, completeness, and reliability of data. High-quality data is essential for accurate analytics and decision-making.

ML algorithms can assess data quality by identifying missing values, duplicates, inconsistencies, and errors. AI can also suggest potential corrections or ways to improve data quality.

Furthermore, AI can be used for data profiling, which involves examining data for patterns, trends, and anomalies. This helps ensure that data is correctly interpreted and used.

Recommendations and personalization

ML algorithms can analyze user behavior to understand their preferences and requirements, personalizing the data catalog experience.

For instance, a recommendation engine can suggest relevant data assets based on a user's past behavior. We can use collaborative filtering to recommend data assets that similar users have found helpful.

In addition, ML can predict what a user will need in the future based on patterns in their past behavior, providing valuable data assets proactively.

Semantic search and natural language querying

AI can significantly enhance the search experience in data catalogs. Semantic search involves understanding the intent behind a search query rather than just matching keywords. This can involve understanding synonyms, context, and even user behavior.

Natural Language Querying (NLQ) allows users to ask questions in natural, everyday language rather than using complex query languages. This is achieved through NLP, a branch of AI that involves understanding, interpreting, and generating human language.

Implementing AI and ML effectively in data cataloging involves continuous monitoring and improvement. It's crucial to train and update models regularly and continuously monitor their performance. Collaboration between diverse teams can help ensure that the catalog meets the needs of all users. Ultimately, AI and ML are tools to assist humans, not replace them, and should be used to enhance human decision-making and productivity.

Key learnings

Data standardization, which modifies data to fit a standard format, is critical for data integration and uniformity.

Creating an effective data schema requires defining tables, fields, and relationships, along with implementing keys, indexes, and data integrity constraints.

Data catalog tools automate aspects of schema creation, making data usage more effective and supporting collaboration.

Tagging systems, designed with clarity, consistency, extensibility, and automation in mind, enhance data discoverability and usability.

Taxonomy systems organize data into systematic hierarchies, improving data navigation and governance.

AI and ML can automate data discovery, enhance metadata management, assess data quality, and provide personalized recommendations, contributing to more efficient data cataloging.

CHAPTER 7

Data Cataloging Tools and Technologies

Commercial data cataloging tools

Commercial data cataloging tools and technologies are complex ecosystems that encapsulate a variety of functionalities, from metadata management to data discovery, governance, and data lineage. Here, we will examine these technologies with a focus on the unique features and potential advantages that each offers.

Alation

Alation is a leading solution in the data cataloging landscape and is often celebrated for its ML capabilities. It uses algorithms to automatically catalog data, learning from users' behaviors and interactions with the data, continually enhancing the metadata repository. This behavioral analysis feature learns from data usage patterns and can predict which data users will need based on their job roles and previous queries, enhancing data discovery.

Furthermore, Alation provides a unique interface for data consumers to collaborate and share their knowledge about data. This knowledge is then added back to the catalog, improving the usability and value of the data. Alation's robust data lineage capabilities ensure users understand the data's origins, dependencies, and potential impacts, fostering trust in data assets.

Alex Augmented Data Catalog

Alex Solutions' Augmented Data Catalog automates time-consuming data governance tasks and facilitates data discovery. It leverages ML and NLP to analyze and interpret data, enabling comprehensive data profiling, quality rule execution, and pattern detection. This tool provides a detailed and unified view of enterprise data assets, enhancing data transparency and compliance, and facilitating effective data stewardship. This can help organizations make data-driven decisions with greater accuracy and confidence.

Ataccama Data Catalog

Ataccama Data Catalog allows users to explore, share, and understand their data through its intuitive self-service interface. The tool is equipped with a metadata scanner that can discover data from various sources and enhance the metadata with additional attributes, inferred relationships, and more. It supports data profiling and provides data quality insights, making it an effective tool for organizations looking to streamline their data governance process.

AWS Glue Data Catalog

AWS Glue Data Catalog, a part of Amazon Web Services, is a fully managed, serverless data catalog that serves as a centralized metadata repository for a wide array of AWS services. It can easily integrate with services like Amazon S3, Amazon RDS, Amazon Redshift, and more, thus providing a unified and comprehensive view of data assets within the AWS ecosystem. Its schema discovery, versioning, and robust metadata search features further enhance its utility in managing and governing data across various AWS services.

Azure Purview

Microsoft Azure Purview is a unified data governance service that enables automated data discovery, cataloging, and end-to-end data lineage. It can create a holistic, multi-cloud, and on-premises data map, providing a unified view of the data landscape. The data cataloging engine uses more than 100 classifiers to discover and classify sensitive data automatically. Integration with Microsoft Power BI and Azure Synapse Analytics ensures data governance across the analytics architecture, making Azure Purview a compelling solution for organizations using the Microsoft technology stack.

Boomi Data Catalog and Preparation

Boomi Data Catalog and Preparation, a part of Boomi's Data Management Suite, focuses on helping users explore, transform, and combine data across the enterprise. Its machine learning-based technology assists in cataloging data, making it easily searchable and discoverable. One of the key strengths of this tool is its ability to prepare data for analysis, combining data quality, enrichment, and transformation capabilities in one solution.

Collibra Catalog

Collibra Catalog excels at helping organizations democratize their data. It offers a centralized location where users can easily find, understand, and trust their data. The user-friendly interface encourages data discovery and collaboration, promoting a data-centric culture within the organization.

A standout feature is its "data scoring" functionality. This feature uses various metrics to calculate the trustworthiness and relevance of datasets, giving users an additional layer of confidence in their data selection. With rich metadata management, lineage tracking, and automated workflows for data stewardship, Collibra presents a comprehensive solution for improving data governance and usage.

data.world

Data.world provides a cloud-native catalog that connects data, metadata, and business context, providing a unified data discovery, governance, and analysis platform. It strongly emphasizes collaboration and knowledge sharing, enabling teams to work together in real-time to query data, share insights, and collaborate on data-related projects. This makes it a highly suitable tool for organizations that value data democratization and collaboration.

Erwin Data Catalog

Erwin Data Catalog, previously known as Erwin Data Intelligence, automates enterprise metadata management, data mapping, code generation, and data lineage. It helps organizations discover and understand data from anywhere, ensuring consistency, clarity, and artifact reuse across large-scale data integration, analytics, data governance, and metadata management initiatives. This facilitates more effective use of data and ensures greater compliance with data-related regulations.

Google Cloud Data Catalog

Google Cloud Data Catalog is a fully managed, scalable data discovery and metadata management service that provides capabilities for automatic metadata ingestion, data discovery, data governance, and rich analytics. It offers a powerful search feature and fine-grained, role-based access control to data metadata. Its integration with Google's data analytics products like BigQuery makes it a seamless and effective tool for organizations operating within the Google Cloud ecosystem.

IBM Watson Knowledge Catalog

IBM Watson Knowledge Catalog provides an intelligent, enterprise-wide data cataloging solution. It offers a unified view of all available data across the organization. One of its distinguishing features is its policy-driven approach to data governance. It can automatically apply data protection rules, ensuring the organization complies with data privacy regulations and security requirements.

Moreover, Watson Knowledge Catalog offers automatic data classification capabilities and AI-powered search functionality. These features allow users to locate and understand their data effectively, reducing the time needed to find valuable insights into the data.

Informatica Enterprise Data Catalog

Informatica EDC is a scalable, enterprise-ready solution with standout AI and ML capabilities. Informatica EDC's strength lies in its ability to automate data discovery, cataloging, and annotation. It offers powerful semantic search capabilities, enabling users to efficiently search and discover suitable datasets.

EDC's unique selling proposition is its CLAIRE engine, an AI/ML-based system that scans and infers relationships and semantic similarities between data across different sources. CLAIRE assists with metadata management and lineage tracing, and it even recommends the most relevant datasets to users based on their usage patterns.

Lumada Data Catalog

Hitachi's Lumada Data Catalog uses machine learning-based asset discovery and automated metadata tagging to optimize data pipeline productivity. It assists in discovering, curating, and democratizing trusted data across silos, providing data intelligence to drive insights. Its ability to organize and manage metadata across various data silos makes it an effective tool for improving data visibility and governance.

Oracle Cloud Infrastructure Data Catalog

Oracle's data catalog offering provides data discovery, governance, and lineage capabilities across Oracle Cloud Infrastructure services. It has automated crawling, entity recognition, and data profiling capabilities. Its powerful search engine helps users quickly find data, improving the efficiency of data discovery. This tool is a fitting choice for organizations that are heavily invested in Oracle's suite of cloud infrastructure services.

OvalEdge

OvalEdge offers a comprehensive data cataloging solution, providing robust metadata management, data governance, data discovery, and data lineage. Its collaboration features encourage a data-driven culture in the organization, fostering better decision-making. Its strong data privacy features, including automated data masking and anonymization, help organizations protect sensitive data, making it a valuable tool for data privacy and compliance.

Qlik Catalog

Qlik Catalog delivers a comprehensive data management solution that automates the discovery, preparation, and delivery of analytics-ready data. Its data catalog indexes and publishes metadata from any source, making it easily discoverable and ready for analysis. The tool's capabilities help streamline data preparation, ensuring data reliability and consistency for downstream analytics applications.

Tableau Catalog

Tableau Catalog, a part of Tableau Data Management, gives visibility and understanding into the data used in Tableau. It automatically keeps track of the relationships between databases, tables, and downstream data sources, workbooks, and dashboards. This visibility, combined with Tableau's powerful visualization capabilities, ensures that users have a comprehensive understanding of their data. This is an excellent choice for organizations that use Tableau for their data visualization needs.

Although this is not a complete list of commercial data cataloging solutions, I have tried to give a spectrum of the key ones that stand out in the industry. Each offers a diverse range of features and capabilities to address data management challenges. The choice between these solutions would depend on the specific needs of an organization. Considerations could include the ease of integration with existing systems, the breadth of support for different data sources, the robustness of data governance capabilities, the efficiency of data discovery and understanding, and the overall user experience. Each offers varied strengths that cater to different organizational needs.

Open-source data cataloging tools

As organizations increasingly understand the value of big data, the importance of data cataloging has grown. However, the wide variety of data formats, types, and storage systems, from cloud-based to on-premise databases, complicate data cataloging efforts. Fortunately, numerous open-source data cataloging tools have emerged to help solve these challenges. These open-source tools allow companies to start with a lower-cost option while also providing the flexibility to modify and customize the tools to fit the specific needs of the organization.

Amundsen

Amundsen, developed and open-sourced by Lyft, is a data discovery and metadata engine for improving the productivity of data analysts, data scientists, and engineers when interacting with data. It utilizes a combination of a search interface, metadata service, and an optional feature of data lineage.

Amundsen integrates with many data sources and catalogs metadata about datasets, including their schema structure, what they are used for, and how frequently they are updated. The data is indexed in Elasticsearch, enabling quick and responsive searches. It also has a PageRank-style algorithm for ranking search results, which promotes more commonly used resources.

Apache Atlas

Apache Atlas is an open-source tool that handles data governance and metadata management challenges. It provides capabilities like data classification, lineage, discovery, and security, all essential for a robust data cataloging tool.

One of the main features of Apache Atlas is its data lineage capability, which offers a visual representation of data flow, helping users understand data origins, transformations, and consumption. It also includes a robust set of REST APIs that allow for easy integration with other tools and systems.

CKAN

CKAN (Comprehensive Knowledge Archive Network) is a powerful open-source data management system that makes data accessible by providing tools to streamline publishing, sharing, finding, and using data. CKAN is aimed at data publishers (national and regional governments, companies, and organizations) wanting to make their data open and available.

CKAN's features include a web-based user interface, a powerful API, data visualization, a data storage system, and more. It supports various types of data, including structured data (like CSV and Excel), geospatial data (like GeoJSON), and unstructured data (like PDFs and Word documents). CKAN is a flexible system that allows organizations to customize the interface and functionality to meet their specific needs.

It is built on a modular architecture, making it easy to plug in extensions or customize the system's behavior. CKAN's core offers a robust API, dataset metadata, and a web interface, but additional features such as data storage, preview, and geospatial handling are all provided by extensions.

DataHub

DataHub, created by LinkedIn, is another open-source metadata management and data discovery tool. It focuses on metadata rather than the data itself, storing and indexing metadata for ease of discovery.

DataHub includes a searchable catalog, a metadata graph for exploring relationships, and an audit trail for tracking changes. It also includes metadata ingestion support from various sources and the ability to extend the schema for new metadata types.

Magda

Magda is an open-source data cataloging system built by the Australian Government's Digital Transformation Agency. It was designed to overcome the challenges of dealing with large amounts of data spread across many different systems, departments, and organizations.

Magda provides a global view of an organization's data, providing a single place to discover datasets regardless of where they are stored or how they are formatted. It focuses on metadata, allowing users to search for datasets, understand what they contain, and determine whether they are suitable for their needs.

Magda is built using a microservices architecture, which makes it highly scalable and allows for rapid feature development. It also features a customizable metadata schema, enabling organizations to define what metadata to capture based on their specific requirements.

It has a built-in crawler that scans and indexes datasets from multiple sources and a search engine built on Elasticsearch. It also provides an intuitive web interface for easy data discovery and exploration.

Metacat

Metacat, open-sourced by Netflix, is a unified metadata exploration API service. It focuses on solving metadata problems for big data workloads, especially in a cloud-based, multi-tenant, and federated environment.

Metacat acts as a federated service, connecting to various data systems, such as SQL, NoSQL, and file-based storage systems. It has a plug-in architecture that allows users to add metadata definitions and services, and it can partition data into logical groupings that are easier to manage. It also provides metadata storage in a pluggable manner, and users can choose their storage backend.

Although this is not a complete list of open-source data cataloging tools, I have tried to give a spectrum of the key ones that stand out. While these open-source data cataloging tools provide numerous benefits, they also have their own complexities and challenges. They require a level of expertise to implement and maintain, and some may not offer all the features needed for a particular use case. Therefore, it's essential for organizations to carefully evaluate these tools, considering factors such as the complexity of their data environment, the specific features they need, and their ability to support and maintain the tool.

Moreover, the open-source nature of these tools provides an opportunity for active contribution and collaboration, encouraging further improvements and advancements in the field of data cataloging.

Evaluating and selecting the right tool

Data cataloging tools are pivotal to an organization's data management and governance strategy. These tools, serving as comprehensive repositories, facilitate data asset discovery, comprehension, and efficient management. Given the plethora of data cataloging tools currently available, choosing the right one can be challenging. This section provides an in-depth approach to guide your selection process.

Understand your requirements

Embarking on the selection process requires, first and foremost, a clear understanding of your organization's needs and the specific problems a data catalog aims to address. Here are some questions that may help delineate your needs:

What kind of data assets does your organization handle, and what's their volume and complexity?

Are you trying to solve problems related to data discovery, data quality, metadata management, data lineage, or data governance?

Do you need collaborative features that allow users to share insights, annotate, and rate data?

What level of automation does your organization require for processes such as metadata ingestion or data classification?

Is compliance with specific regulations (e.g., GDPR, HIPAA) a significant factor?

List the key features and functionalities your organization needs before exploring the offerings of different tools.

Technical compatibility

Consider whether the data cataloging tool is compatible with your existing tech stack. It should seamlessly integrate with the databases, data warehouses, ETL tools, BI platforms, and other software already in use within your organization. The tool should support your data sources, which could be SQL or NoSQL databases, cloud-based sources, on-premises, or hybrid data environments. Also, consider future technical needs as your organization evolves and expands its tech stack.

Usability and user interface

An intuitive, user-friendly tool encourages adoption across your organization, making it accessible to a broad spectrum of users – from data scientists to business analysts. Evaluate the tool's usability in terms of ease of navigation, data discovery, visualization features, and learning curve. Features such as a search bar, tagging, rating systems, and user-friendly visualization of complex data relationships can significantly improve the user experience and increase efficiency.

Data governance and security

Comprehensive data governance capabilities are a must for data cataloging tools. Automated data classification, robust metadata management, data lineage tracing, and a business glossary aid in understanding and controlling data assets. A business glossary, for instance, ensures that all users have a common understanding of business terms and metrics.

In terms of security, the tool should offer role-based access control to manage who can view and edit data. Encryption of sensitive data, regular audit trails, and features to manage regulatory compliance are also essential to protect your data assets and avoid legal complications.

Scalability

As your organization and data grow, the chosen tool should be able to scale with it. It should handle an increasing volume of data and greater complexity without a drop in performance. Consider the tool's architecture – does it support distributed processing, can it handle real-time data updates, and does it allow for scalability without significant disruptions or high costs?

Vendor support

Quality of vendor support is an essential consideration. Post-purchase services such as technical assistance, user training, and regular software updates significantly contribute to the tool's usability and overall satisfaction. Assessing the vendor's market reputation, longevity, and financial stability is also essential.

Pricing

While quality should not be compromised for cost, the pricing model of the tool should align with your budgetary constraints. Understand the pricing model – is it a one-time purchase, a subscription-based model, or a pay-as-you-go model? Also, consider the total cost of ownership, which includes not only the price of the software but also costs related to implementation, maintenance, training, and potential future upgrades.

Proof of concept

After shortlisting potential data cataloging tools that meet your criteria, run a proof of concept (PoC) to assess their performance in a real-world scenario. A PoC can help you verify if the tool meets your specific needs, works well with your data ecosystem, and is easy for your team to use.

Review process

It can be beneficial to establish a review process that includes stakeholders from different departments – IT, data governance, business units, and legal. This diverse perspective can help ensure that the chosen tool meets a wide range of needs and expectations.

Selecting the correct data cataloging tool is a nuanced process that requires a deep understanding of your organization's unique needs, technical infrastructure, and budget. The chosen tool should be capable of managing your data ecosystem's complexities while ensuring robust data governance and security and remain scalable and adaptable in the face of organizational growth and evolving needs.

Key learnings

Open-source data cataloging tools provide alternative solutions, especially pertinent for organizations mindful of technical and budgetary considerations.

Vendor support, especially focusing on post-purchase services like technical assistance and user training, plays a critical role in ensuring the smooth adoption and sustained utilization of a tool.

An in-depth understanding of pricing models and total cost of ownership is fundamental to ensuring the chosen tool aligns with the organization's budget and financial sustainability expectations.

Implementing a Proof of Concept (PoC) is crucial to assess the real-world performance of a tool, ensuring it can effectively meet the operational demands and practical necessities of an organization.

The chosen tool should not only manage complexities and assure robust data governance and security but also exhibit scalability and adaptability to support organizational growth and evolving data needs.

PART IV

Implementing and Maintaining a Data Catalog

CHAPTER 8

Data Cataloging Strategy and Planning

When planning your data cataloging strategy, the first and most essential step is the assessment of your organization's data cataloging requirements. We should not undertake this process lightly, as it sets the foundation for your future work and ultimately influences the effectiveness and utility of your data catalog. The assessment stage will help you determine what kind of data you have, where it is, who uses it, what it is used for, and more.

Understanding your organization's data landscape is a multifaceted process that requires concerted efforts from different sectors of the organization. You need to identify all data sources, repositories, and databases that store data. This includes structured databases, unstructured data sources such as documents, data warehouses, data lakes, and even external data sources used by the organization. To build a comprehensive list, you need to work closely with data owners, data stewards, IT, and other stakeholders who manage these data sources. Collaborating with these individuals provides critical context about each data source, including the type of data stored, format, volume, update frequency, and usage.

Data usage analysis

Understanding how data is used in your organization will inform which datasets are most crucial and how to prioritize their cataloging. This analysis involves identifying key data users and their roles, determining which data they use, how they use it, their existing pain points, and how a data catalog could aid in their work.

This analysis might involve surveys, interviews, or workshops with key data users. Users might include data scientists, analysts, decision-makers, and operational teams. Their input will help you understand critical datasets, common data usage patterns, and crucial metadata needed in the catalog. Moreover, it allows you to recognize areas where data usage could be improved with better data accessibility and understanding.

Data governance policies and data catalog alignment

Your data cataloging strategy should reflect and support your organization's data governance policies. These policies often encompass a wide range of aspects, including data quality, data privacy, data security, data lifecycle management, and regulatory compliance. You must understand these policies thoroughly and how they apply to different datasets.

Consider, for instance, data privacy and security. If certain data sets contain sensitive data, you need to ensure your data cataloging strategy accounts for this. It might mean implementing data masking, data anonymization, or other security controls within the data catalog.

Regulatory compliance

Depending on your industry, your organization might be subject to data-related regulations such as GDPR, CCPA, HIPAA, or industry-specific regulations. These regulations might impose specific requirements for data cataloging. For example, GDPR requires organizations to document what personal data they hold, where it came from, who it's shared with, and how it's used. Therefore, your data catalog might need to capture this information.

Ensure that your data cataloging strategy addresses these regulatory requirements and consider how your data catalog could help demonstrate compliance. For instance, you might want to incorporate automatic detection and tagging of sensitive data, provide clear data lineage, maintain audit logs, or offer functionality for data rights management.

Technological capabilities and constraints

Evaluating your organization's technological capabilities and constraints will guide the practical implementation of your data cataloging strategy. This evaluation should consider the existing data architecture, the software and hardware infrastructure, the technical skills of your team, and the budget available for data cataloging efforts. This understanding will guide your choice of a data catalog solution. For instance, if your organization uses a heterogeneous mix of data sources, you might need a data catalog tool with robust integration capabilities. Conversely, if your team lacks advanced technical skills, a more user-friendly data catalog tool with solid customer support might be more appropriate.

Stakeholder needs and expectations

Finally, engaging with various stakeholders will help you understand their needs and expectations from a data catalog. While the needs of data users are crucial, other stakeholders like senior management, regulatory authorities, and even customers might also have essential perspectives. These perspectives will inform your data cataloging strategy, ensuring it delivers value across the organization and beyond.

Assessing data cataloging requirements is a foundational step that shapes your data cataloging strategy and determines its effectiveness. This comprehensive assessment ensures that your data catalog is well-equipped to support your organization's data governance and data utilization objectives, creating a data-centric culture that accelerates data-driven decision-making.

Developing a data cataloging roadmap

Formulating a comprehensive data cataloging roadmap is a crucial part of any data governance program, as it defines the strategic direction for a business in its pursuit of valuable insights and data-driven decision-making. This roadmap can enhance the organization's capacity to identify, understand, and utilize its data assets more effectively. This section will explore the key steps and considerations in developing a data cataloging roadmap.

Establish the vision

A successful data cataloging initiative starts with a clearly defined vision that links with your organization's overall data strategy. This vision could involve improving data discoverability, enhancing data privacy compliance, or enabling advanced analytics.

The vision will act as a guiding principle for all data cataloging efforts and should be communicated to all stakeholders to ensure alignment. Importantly, it should be flexible enough to adapt to changing business needs and regulatory requirements.

Define the scope

Your data cataloging initiative could encompass a wide range of data sources, from traditional databases and data warehouses to more recent additions like big data systems and cloud repositories. Decide which data sources and types to begin cataloging based on their relevance to your business goals, data quality, and ease of integration. Some organizations may start with high-value or high-risk datasets, while others might prioritize based on the data's visibility and accessibility.

Assess current state

Before any improvements can be made, you must conduct an in-depth evaluation of your current data landscape. This involves identifying all available data sources, noting their location, data format, and access methods, and understanding the quality of the data they hold. Take note of any existing data catalogs, metadata management tools, data dictionaries, or other data management solutions currently in place. Evaluate them in terms of their effectiveness, usage, and satisfaction among end users.

Gap analysis

Perform a comprehensive gap analysis to understand the difference between your current state and your envisioned state of data cataloging. This analysis should highlight weaknesses in current systems, such as inconsistent metadata, poor data quality, inadequate data security, or limited access to data.

The gap analysis should be carried out across multiple dimensions – people, processes, technology, and data. This will help in identifying both the technical and non-technical improvements needed.

Select data cataloging tool

Selecting the correct data cataloging tool is a crucial decision that can significantly influence the success of your data cataloging efforts. Consider factors like the tool's ability to handle different types of data and metadata, scalability as your data grows, capacity for automation, compliance features, and integration capabilities with other data management systems in your organization. Also, consider the tool's user interface and ease of use, as it needs to be accessible to a wide range of users, from data scientists and analysts to business users.

Define metadata management strategy

A well-defined metadata management strategy is at the heart of a successful data catalog. It involves defining how metadata is captured, stored, and accessed across the organization. Your strategy should cover the management of different types of metadata, as detailed in Chapter 5, *Data Profiling and Data Discovery*. Consider using standards like ISO 11179 or Dublin Core for metadata management.

Prioritize and plan implementation

After the gap analysis, prioritize the improvements based on their impact on your vision, their feasibility, and their alignment with your business strategy. It is usually advisable to start with quick wins to gain momentum and prove value.

The implementation should be phased to minimize disruption. Each phase could target a specific dataset or business area. Include milestones and checkpoints to measure progress and adjust the plan if necessary.

Define roles and responsibilities

The data cataloging initiative will require collaboration across different roles – data owners who are responsible for the data's accuracy and usage, data stewards who maintain the data catalog, data architects who design the data structure, and data privacy officers who ensure compliance with regulations.

These roles should be clearly defined and communicated to avoid confusion and overlaps. Training may be required to equip team members with the necessary skills.

Establish data quality measures

The effectiveness of a data catalog largely depends on the quality of the underlying data. Establish measures for data quality, such as accuracy, completeness, consistency, and timeliness.

Implement processes and tools to monitor data quality continuously, flag issues, and initiate remedial actions. Automating these checks can save time and ensure reliability.

Regular review and improvement

The data landscape is constantly changing, with new data sources being added and existing ones evolving. The data cataloging roadmap should include provisions for regular reviews and updates to the catalog to reflect these changes.

It is also crucial to solicit feedback from users and stakeholders and make necessary improvements. The success of the data cataloging initiative should be measured based on predefined KPIs and reported to the stakeholders.

By following these steps and taking a strategic, thorough, and adaptive approach, organizations can develop a robust data cataloging roadmap that meets their unique needs and drives their data governance initiatives forward.

Budgeting and resource allocation

A practical data cataloging strategy, properly budgeted and resourced, is critical to ensure data quality, governance, and value extraction. Developing a comprehensive budgeting plan and resource allocation spans financial, human, technological, and temporal considerations. Budgeting includes:

- **Initial investment**. The journey begins with an initial investment in a suitable data cataloging tool. A diverse range of such tools, each offering a variety of features, functionalities, and pricing models, is available in the market. The choice should be driven by the organization's unique needs, existing data infrastructure, and strategic data goals. Additionally, this budget should consider any necessary hardware upgrades to support the newly introduced software. Keep in mind that costs are not just product costs. Factor in expenses for the implementation of the tool, which may include data migration, system configuration, integration with existing systems, and preliminary testing.

- **Ongoing expenses**. Operational costs are recurring and should be factored into the budgeting plan. These cover expenses related to software updates, preventive maintenance, troubleshooting, and potential expansion of the data cataloging tool. Vendor subscription fees, costs associated with cloud storage or data warehousing, or any other associated recurring costs should be included.

- **Training and support**. Allocating a budget for training and support is essential to realize the full potential of your data cataloging tool. Employees need to be thoroughly familiar with the tool's functionalities and best practices for it to be effectively utilized. This may involve the cost of internal training sessions, external courses, or hiring a consultant for a comprehensive training process. Remember to account for ongoing support costs, too.

- **Data governance**. A considerable portion of your budget should be set aside for establishing and maintaining robust data governance frameworks and practices. This includes resources for data stewardship, ensuring data quality, preserving data privacy, and meeting compliance requirements.

Resources include:

- **Human resources**. Data cataloging is not a one-person show. A well-rounded team of data professionals is pivotal to ensuring effective data cataloging. Key roles typically include data engineers, data analysts, data stewards, and data governance officers. Depending on your operations' scale, you may need multiple personnel in these roles. Factor in the cost of sourcing and retaining these professionals, which may include competitive salaries, benefits, and professional development opportunities. Also, consider the need for cross-training existing staff members to foster a data-aware culture.

- **Technological resources**. Technological resources form the backbone of your data cataloging strategy. These comprise hardware, software, and IT infrastructure essential for data cataloging. The requirements may include high-performance servers for processing, data storage solutions, network infrastructure, and necessary software licenses. Moreover, allocate resources for implementing robust security measures to safeguard your data and maintain regulatory compliance. This may involve advanced security software, encryption tools, and intrusion detection systems.

- **Time**. It is vital to acknowledge that implementing a data cataloging strategy is not an instantaneous process. It requires a significant investment of time. Ensure you allocate adequate time for various stages such as tool selection, system design, data ingestion, metadata extraction, data profiling, tool implementation, exhaustive testing, and employee training.

Strategic resource planning includes:

- **Cost-benefit analysis**. Conduct a comprehensive cost-benefit analysis to justify your investment in data cataloging. This analysis should balance both tangible benefits, like improved process efficiency, risk reduction, and compliance adherence, against intangible benefits, such as enhanced decision-making ability, better customer insights, and knowledge sharing.

- **Scalability** The resources allocated should be scalable to accommodate the dynamic nature of data. As the business grows and evolves, the data cataloging strategy should adapt efficiently, scaling up or down as required —budget for periodic review and upgrades of your data cataloging tools and practices.

- **Contingency planning**. Ensure contingency plans are in place to ensure the system's stability and minimize downtime. This might include having a buffer in the budget for unexpected costs, planning for technical glitches, delays in the implementation timeline, or even changes in data regulations.

Budgeting and resource allocation for data cataloging is a multifaceted process that demands strategic planning and meticulous analysis. By allocating appropriate time, money, and personnel for data cataloging, organizations can extract maximum value from their data, creating a efficient, effective, and future-proof strategy.

Key learnings

A thorough assessment of an organization's data cataloging requirements is crucial for the future effectiveness of the data catalog.

Analyzing how we use data within the organization can help prioritize the cataloging of critical datasets.

The data cataloging strategy should align with the organization's data governance policies, including data quality, data privacy, data security, and regulatory compliance.

Security considerations, especially with sensitive data, should be incorporated into the data cataloging strategy.

The data cataloging strategy is a foundational process that sets the stage for future work.

CHAPTER 9

Data Cataloging Implementation

Data cataloging has become an increasingly significant practice for businesses managing large amounts of data. A data catalog allows organizations to locate, understand, and use their data more effectively by creating a single source of reference for all data assets.

Data cataloging process

This section will delve into the technical aspects of data cataloging implementation, with a particular emphasis on the data cataloging process.

Process initiation

This is the initial phase of the data cataloging process. Here, the data cataloging system is sparked into action either through a manual start initiated by a user or an automatic one, like an event trigger. For instance, an event like an update in a data source or adding a new data source can initiate the data cataloging system. The configuration of these triggers needs to be meticulously arranged according to the data lifecycle within the organization.

Data ingestion and metadata extraction

In this step, data is ingested from the identified sources, and metadata is extracted. A variety of tasks, such as data extract, transform, and load, and metadata extraction, take place at this stage. These tasks might run concurrently or sequentially, depending on the architectural design. The process here involves efficient scheduling of these tasks, error handling, and retry mechanisms to ensure accurate data and metadata extraction.

Task assignment for classification & categorization

Once the ingestion is complete, the process moves on to the assignment of classification and categorization tasks. Based on the complexity of data and business needs, these tasks could be assigned to ML algorithms for automatic classification or to human operators for manual classification. The process manages the assignment of these tasks, monitors their progress, handles reprioritization of tasks, and ensures proper completion.

Synchronization with data profiling

The data cataloging process synchronizes with the data profiling system. This system generates statistics and insights concurrently by analyzing the data. We should design the process to handle this synchronization, ensuring no data conflicts and that the catalog is updated with the most recent profiling information.

Implementation of data governance

At this stage, we apply data governance rules to the data. The process manages the triggering of scripts or functions that ensure data compliance with various regulations, setting access permissions, data lineage documentation, and more. This stage can be complex as it involves cross-functional collaboration and must balance data accessibility with security and compliance.

Regular updates and maintenance

The process includes scheduling regular updates and maintenance tasks to keep the data catalog accurate and up-to-date. This involves creating a system to monitor for changes in data sources, detect issues in data quality, handle exceptions, and perform corrections. The process must manage these tasks efficiently to ensure data integrity.

End-user interface interaction

The process also manages interactions with the end-user interface, ensuring that updates are accurately reflected in the user-facing aspects of the catalog. User queries should be efficiently handled, and search results accurately provided. The process needs to integrate user feedback mechanisms and handle updates and enhancements to the user interface.

Monitoring and improvement

The final part of the data cataloging process involves constant monitoring of the entire procedure to identify bottlenecks, inefficiencies, or potential improvements. It should leverage ML and AI to refine the process continuously and use analytics to provide insights into usage patterns, data quality, and user behavior. This stage ensures the overall data cataloging process's scalability, robustness, and efficiency.

The data cataloging process comprehensively orchestrates multiple distinct steps into a seamless operation. It manages the entire life cycle of data within the catalog, from initial ingestion and metadata extraction, through classification, categorization, and governance, to user interface interaction and ongoing maintenance, with a constant emphasis on monitoring and improvement.

Data ingestion and indexing

Creating an effective data catalog system requires a comprehensive approach to data ingestion and indexing. These processes together enable the data to be organized, accessible, and retrievable. Below, we will explore these concepts in even greater depth, covering a broader range of techniques, challenges, and best practices.

Data ingestion entails the process of gathering, importing, and processing data for storage or immediate use. It forms the groundwork for data cataloging and governs how different types of data are brought into the system. Data ingestion techniques include:

- **Batch metadata ingestion**. It involves importing metadata in bulk at predetermined intervals. This can be useful for data catalogs that need to ingest large volumes of metadata from data warehouses or other sources where data is loaded in batches.

- **Stream metadata ingestion**. It involves importing metadata in real-time as it is generated. This is necessary for data catalogs that need to stay up-to-date with real-time data sources.

- **Hybrid metadata ingestion**. Combines batch and stream ingestion to offer the most comprehensive and up-to-date metadata collection. This is useful for data catalogs that include both batch-loaded and real-time data sources.

Each of these techniques can be facilitated with a range of tools. Apache NiFi or Apache Kafka can be configured to collect metadata, while specific data catalog tools, like Google Cloud Data Catalog, automatically collect metadata during data ingestion.

There are challenges to data ingestion:

- **Data variety**. The variety of data formats, from structured (SQL, CSV) to semi-structured (XML, JSON) and unstructured data (emails, documents), increases the complexity of the ingestion process.

- **Volume and scalability**. Organizations often grapple with handling massive amounts of data while ensuring efficient scalability.

- **Data quality**. A significant challenge lies in maintaining the quality and accuracy of ingested data and dealing with duplicates, errors, or inconsistent formats.

Follow these data ingestion best practices:

- **Automation**. Leverage ETL tools or similar data pipeline technologies to automate data ingestion.

- **Monitoring and logging**. Monitor data ingestion pipelines continuously to identify and address failures promptly.

- **Data validation**. Employ data validation checks to ensure ingested data adheres to defined quality standards.

- **Data Indexing**. Data indexing involves mapping data to create indexes that allow faster data retrieval. It dramatically enhances query performance and provides structure to the data in the catalog.

Indexing in a data catalog context refers to the process of organizing metadata to enable efficient metadata retrieval. There are different types of indexing:

- **Keyword-based indexing**. Much like a book index, this involves indexing the metadata based on specific keywords. Users can quickly locate data assets related to a particular term or phrase.

- **Faceted indexing**. It involves indexing metadata based on various "facets" or categories. For example, we might categorize data by its source, type, owner, or creation date. This is useful for users who want to explore data based on specific characteristics.

- **Relationship-based indexing.** It involves creating indexes that reflect the relationships between different data assets. This is particularly useful for complex data environments where understanding the relationships between data can provide valuable context.

- **Full-text indexing.** It involves creating an index of all the words in the metadata. This allows for powerful search functionality, enabling users to locate data assets based on any term included in the metadata.

Many tools are available for indexing metadata within a data catalog, ranging from open-source solutions like Elasticsearch to commercial offerings, such as Alation's data catalog. Data indexing challenges include:

- **Space management.** While beneficial for retrieval, indexing consumes disk space and could create storage constraints.

- **Performance.** Achieving the balance between the improved performance of query operations and the overhead of maintaining indexes during data modifications can be challenging.

- **Complexity.** Developing and managing indexes across different types of data sources and data formats involve significant complexity.

Following these data indexing best practices:

- **Selective indexing**. Index only those columns that are often involved in search or filter operations to optimize performance.

- **Regular maintenance**. Regular index maintenance and optimization are essential to ensure that they continue to deliver performance gains.

- **Monitor performance**. Continually monitor the performance of the system to understand whether indexes are improving or hindering query performance.

The techniques used for data ingestion and indexing in a data cataloging context are tailored to the unique requirements of managing metadata. They allow for a comprehensive, searchable, and highly organized data catalog that can serve as a valuable resource for any data-driven organization.

Hybrid and multi-cloud environments

The data management landscape has significantly shifted in the last decade, with hybrid and multi-cloud environments becoming more prevalent due to their flexibility, scalability, and cost-effectiveness. This shift presents a multitude of challenges, particularly in the area of data cataloging. Data cataloging involves organizing, classifying, and indexing datasets to create an easily searchable repository and is a crucial part of an organization's data governance strategy.

In hybrid and multi-cloud environments, data sources are distributed, making it complex to maintain an updated and unified view of the data. Therefore, a practical data cataloging strategy and its successful implementation are essential in such environments to leverage the full potential of data.

Data source variability

In a hybrid or multi-cloud environment, data can reside in various locations – on-premises or in different public or private clouds. Each location can have a diverse range of data sources, like databases, data lakes, data warehouses, or even flat files. This diversity can create complexities while cataloging, as different data sources may have unique metadata, formats, and structures.

Data governance and security

Data governance involves the overall management of data availability, usability, integrity, and security. It is a more significant challenge in hybrid and multi-cloud environments due to the fragmentation of data. Security policies and access controls may differ from one cloud provider to another, creating potential risks.

Data silos

Hybrid and multi-cloud environments can unintentionally encourage data silos. If data is stored separately without proper metadata management, it can become isolated and inaccessible to other parts of the organization, thereby limiting the insights that can be derived.

The successful implementation of data cataloging in hybrid and multi-cloud environments is complex but critical to ensuring an organization can fully leverage its data assets. It involves addressing several challenges, from data source variability to data governance.

By standardizing metadata, implementing a centralized data catalog, applying uniform security and governance policies, and utilizing automation, organizations can create a robust data cataloging system that enhances data discoverability, usability, and governance.

Key learnings

The process of data cataloging heavily relies on effective data ingestion, particularly metadata ingestion. Addressing challenges in batch processes is crucial for a smooth cataloging process.

Data governance plays a significant role in managing and utilizing data assets effectively. A well-structured cataloging process is pivotal for successful data governance.

The efficiency of data retrieval from the catalog can be significantly enhanced by focusing on performance, mainly through effective indexing based on specific parameters.

Regular maintenance and operation following best practices are essential to ensure the effectiveness and reliability of data catalogs over time.

Metadata plays a critical role in data cataloging tasks. A systematic process for managing and integrating metadata into the data catalog is crucial for successful data cataloging.

CHAPTER 10

Metadata Harvesting and Automation

The role of metadata in the digital landscape can't be overstated. It's a rich, contextual source of information that enhances the discoverability, accessibility, and usability of data. Within the domain of data catalog metadata harvesting and automation, this is particularly evident. This process involves two essential tasks: crawling and extracting metadata. Let's delve into the intricacies of these tasks and their broader implications in data catalog management.

Crawling in data catalogs

Firstly, it's crucial to define what a "crawl" means in this context. Essentially, crawling is the systematic browsing of network resources to scan and identify data assets. The goal is to map a given network's data landscape. In a data catalog, this is often performed by a crawler, an automated program or script that systematically browses the network, exploring databases, file systems, and data lakes, among others. It's important to note that effective crawling is not simply about locating data but also involves understanding its structure and format.

Data catalog crawlers must be able to handle a wide array of data sources, formats, and schemas, recognizing the critical metadata attributes in each. They may need to navigate through structured databases like SQL or Oracle, semi-structured data formats like JSON or XML, unstructured data sources like text documents, or big data systems like Hadoop HDFS and Apache Cassandra. These crawlers use connection details provided by the user (like connection strings or access keys) to connect to these sources and initiate the metadata harvesting process.

Extracting metadata

Upon discovering a data source, the crawler begins to inspect its structure and content to extract metadata. The extraction process varies depending on the type of data source. For instance, in relational databases, the crawler may inspect tables, views, columns, data types, indexes, constraints, stored procedures, and other elements to extract metadata. It may also collect statistics such as row counts or data distributions. In a file system, the crawler may inspect directories and files, extracting metadata like file names, sizes, creation dates, and more. In big data systems, the crawler may inspect datasets, their schema, and associated metadata.

Metadata extraction, thus, is a process of collecting, organizing, and storing data about data. However, it's not only about collecting raw technical metadata but also includes extracting business metadata (like data ownership, data stewardship, and business definitions) and operational metadata (like data quality scores and data lineage). Extracting this kind of metadata empowers users to understand the data at a deeper level, beyond its surface information, improving the data's findability, understandability, and trust.

Automation in metadata harvesting

The extraction of metadata is a crucial step for creating an active and usable data catalog. This metadata helps data consumers locate suitable datasets, understand their structure, evaluate their quality, and determine their appropriateness for a particular use case. However, it's also necessary to ensure that the metadata is consistently, accurately captured, and updated, which is where automation comes in.

Automation is a vital part of metadata harvesting as it can ensure that metadata is consistently captured and kept up-to-date, enabling real-time or near real-time cataloging of data assets. Manual metadata collection and cataloging can be time-consuming, error-prone, and not scalable, particularly in today's big data environments where data volumes, velocity, and variety continue to grow. Automated crawlers can run on a scheduled basis or in response to triggers like changes in data sources. They can identify new data assets, changes to existing ones, and capture this information automatically.

In the context of automation, incremental crawling is an essential strategy. Rather than crawling the entire data landscape every time, incremental crawlers focus on what's changed since the last crawl, thus reducing resource usage and ensuring timely updates. This is particularly relevant in big data systems, where a full crawl can be resource-intensive and time-consuming.

Moreover, automation enables continuous metadata extraction, which is vital in an environment where data changes frequently. This includes not only technical changes (like changes to schema or data structures) but also business changes (like changes to data ownership or business definitions). By continuously updating the metadata, automated crawlers ensure that the data catalog always reflects the current state of the data landscape.

Crawling and extracting metadata in the context of data catalog metadata harvesting and automation is a multifaceted task that involves the systematic scanning of data sources, the extraction of valuable metadata from those sources, and the automated, consistent capture and updating of that metadata. It's a complex task but one that is essential for effective data catalog management. By improving the discoverability, accessibility, and usability of data, it empowers organizations to harness their data more effectively and make data-driven decisions with greater confidence.

Automated metadata updates and synchronization

Before we delve into the specifics, it is essential to understand why metadata is important and why its automation is necessary. Metadata provides context to data, without which it would be impossible to interpret and utilize data effectively. It aids data governance, data quality control, data lineage tracking, and overall data management. However, given the volume, velocity, and variety of data that organizations generate and handle, manual metadata management becomes infeasible and error-prone.

Automated metadata updates and synchronization systems address these issues by ensuring metadata is accurate, up-to-date, and synchronized across the data catalog. They help organizations maintain a robust, searchable, and efficient data catalog, enabling data users to find and understand data for their needs, whether that's analytics, reporting, ML, or decision-making.

Automated metadata harvesting

Automated metadata harvesting is the process of collecting metadata from various data sources and integrating it into the data catalog. In this context, data sources can be databases, data warehouses, data lakes, or even APIs, each with its unique metadata structure.

A crucial aspect of metadata harvesting is the ability to connect with different types of data sources. This requires an array of connectors designed to interface with each type of source system, understanding its data structures and extracting the metadata. A good metadata harvesting tool will provide out-of-the-box connectors for a variety of familiar data sources and also allow the creation of custom connectors for proprietary or less common systems.

The metadata extraction should ideally be incremental, where after the initial extraction, only changes are extracted during each subsequent run. This reduces the load on the source systems and keeps the metadata in the catalog up-to-date.

Automated metadata updates

After the metadata is harvested and stored in the data catalog, it must be kept up-to-date to reflect changes in the source systems. Data evolves over time. New data may be added, existing data may be updated or deleted, and data schemas may change. These changes need to be reflected in the metadata stored in the data catalog to maintain its accuracy and reliability.

Automated metadata updates address this requirement. They use various techniques such as event-driven updates, periodic polling, and change data capture to identify changes in the source systems and update the metadata in the data catalog accordingly.

Event-driven updates use triggers in the source systems to initiate metadata updates when data changes occur. Periodic polling involves checking the source systems at regular intervals for changes, while change data capture involves tracking changes in the source systems in near-real-time and updating the metadata accordingly.

Metadata synchronization

Automated metadata synchronization is another crucial aspect of maintaining a reliable and efficient data catalog. It ensures that metadata is consistent across different parts of the data catalog and between the catalog and the source systems.

Consistency across the data catalog is crucial when data is replicated or moved between different systems. For example, a table from a production database might be replicated to a data warehouse for reporting purposes. In this case, the metadata for the table in the data warehouse should match that in the production database. Automated metadata synchronization tools can monitor these processes and update the metadata as needed.

Consistency between the data catalog and the source systems is also essential to ensure the catalog accurately represents the data in the sources. If a source system changes (e.g., a column is added to a database table), the catalog's metadata should be updated to reflect this. Automated metadata synchronization tools can track these changes and update the catalog metadata, maintaining a 'single source of truth' for data users.

Implementing automated metadata updates and synchronization isn't without its challenges. Differences in metadata structures across source systems, security, and privacy concerns, performance impacts on source systems, and ensuring data and metadata consistency can all pose difficulties.

The first challenge is dealing with different metadata structures. While some data sources follow standard metadata structures (e.g., SQL databases), others have unique or proprietary structures (e.g., NoSQL databases or certain APIs). To overcome this, organizations may need to develop custom connectors or scripts to extract and interpret metadata from these sources.

Security and privacy are also significant concerns. Metadata often contains sensitive information about data, so access to it needs to be controlled and audited. Additionally, the metadata harvesting and updating process should not expose the source systems to unnecessary risks.

Performance impact on source systems is another consideration. Metadata extraction, particularly the initial extraction, can be resource-intensive. This is especially true for large, active systems where performance impacts could disrupt normal operations. To mitigate this, organizations can schedule metadata extraction during off-peak hours or use incremental extraction techniques to reduce the load.

Ensuring consistency of data and metadata across different systems can also be challenging, especially in complex environments with multiple data sources, replicas, and movements. Here, automated metadata synchronization tools can be invaluable, monitoring data movements and updates, and ensuring that metadata remains consistent across the systems.

Automated metadata updates and synchronization are critical aspects of maintaining a reliable, efficient, and usable data catalog. By harvesting metadata from various data sources, keeping it updated with changes, and ensuring its consistency, organizations can provide a 'single source of truth' about their data, empowering users to find, understand, and effectively utilize data. While implementation may have its challenges, the benefits of improved data governance, data quality, and data usage are undeniable.

Data lineage and impact analysis

Data governance is increasingly important in today's data-driven business environment, making the concept of data lineage and impact analysis particularly relevant. To shed light on these concepts, it's essential, first, to understand the notion of a data catalog, the role metadata plays, and how it interacts with automation processes.

A data catalog serves as a comprehensive inventory of data assets in an organization, providing visibility into where data comes from (source), where it's going (destination), and how it changes as it flows through systems (transformation). The data catalog's ability to provide this level of detail depends largely on metadata. Metadata harvesting refers to the automatic or semi-automatic collection and management of this metadata, often performed by automated processes that identify, extract, and catalog it.

Data lineage and impact analysis come into play as the methods to trace data's lifecycle and assess its potential effects on various systems or business operations, respectively. Both are crucial to efficient data catalog metadata harvesting and automation.

Data lineage

Data lineage refers to the life cycle of data, including its origins, movements, characteristics, and quality. It provides visibility into the entire journey of data from its source to its various points of use. This end-to-end view helps organizations maintain regulatory compliance, enhance data quality, support data integration, and enable root-cause analysis.

We can visualize data lineage as a directed graph, where nodes represent data entities and edges represent transformations. It is a fundamental component of metadata harvesting as it provides information about:

- **Origin**. Where does the data come from? Is it from an external or internal source? Is it from a structured database or an unstructured dataset? Knowing the origin of data allows organizations to assess data reliability and authenticity.

- **Movement.** How does the data travel through the system? This involves understanding all transformations that the data undergo, whether it's simple operations like filtering or complex ones like aggregations or calculations.

- **Usage.** Where and how is the data being used? This includes identifying which business processes or reports use the data. It can also uncover any unauthorized or inappropriate usage of data.

By automating the harvesting of metadata related to data lineage, organizations can maintain up-to-date information about their data's life cycle and ensure timely decision-making.

Impact analysis

While data lineage is about tracing the path of data, impact analysis aims to understand the potential consequences of changes to data or related systems. It's an essential step in risk management, allowing organizations to evaluate and plan for the possible outcomes of a data change.

Impact analysis uses the harvested metadata to answer questions like:

What would happen if a specific data source were to change?

By evaluating how data from the source is used, you can predict the ripple effects a change would have across various business operations.

Which systems would be affected if a particular data transformation were to be modified?

By understanding the dependencies of different transformations, you can gauge the impact a change would have on downstream systems or processes. Automating impact analysis with the help of metadata harvesting can not only help organizations plan for potential risks but also optimize data processes and improve resource allocation.

Data catalog metadata harvesting and automation

Metadata harvesting is critical in populating a data catalog. It involves identifying, extracting, and cataloging metadata from various data sources. The process can be labor-intensive and error-prone when done manually. Therefore, automation plays a vital role.

Automation of metadata harvesting streamlines the process, reducing the chances of errors and ensuring comprehensive and consistent metadata collection. Automated processes can extract various types of metadata, such as administrative technical metadata (e.g., data types, column names), descriptive metadata (e.g., business terms, definitions), and structural metadata (e.g., data lineage, data quality rules).

Automation can also be leveraged to keep the data catalog up-to-date. This involves ongoing monitoring of data sources and transformations to ensure any changes are accurately reflected in the catalog. For instance, if a new data source is added or an existing transformation is changed, the automated system can detect these changes and update the metadata in the catalog accordingly.

Linking data lineage, impact analysis, and automation

Data lineage and impact analysis are interwoven with the process of metadata harvesting and automation. The data lineage information provides an understanding of the data's journey, while the impact analysis leverages this information to predict the possible effects of changes to the data or systems.

Automating these processes enables organizations to keep their data catalogs current and valuable. This automation not only saves time and effort but also enhances data governance by providing consistent, accurate, and timely information about data assets.

Data lineage and impact analysis are crucial to the functioning of a robust data catalog. They enable organizations to maintain visibility into their data's journey and understand the potential impact of changes, respectively. When combined with the power of metadata harvesting and automation, these capabilities empower organizations to effectively govern their data assets, enhance data quality, and make informed, data-driven decisions.

Key learnings

Metadata harvesting is critical for populating a data catalog. This involves collecting metadata from various data sources and integrating it into the data catalog.

Automated metadata harvesting is essential. Data sources can include databases, data warehouses, data lakes, or even APIs, each with its unique metadata structure.

Metadata extraction involves collecting, organizing, and storing data about data. This process is not limited to administrative technical metadata; it also includes the extraction of descriptive metadata (like data ownership, data stewardship, and business definitions) and structural metadata (like data quality scores and data lineage).

Harvesting metadata from various data sources, keeping it updated with changes, and ensuring its consistency allows organizations to provide a 'single source of truth' about their data. This empowers users to find, understand, and effectively utilize data.

Metadata aids in data governance, data quality control, data lineage tracking, and overall data management. Both metadata harvesting and automation are crucial to efficient data catalog metadata harvesting and automation.

CHAPTER 11

Data Cataloging for Big Data and Streaming Data

The revolution of big data and streaming data is indisputably one of the most significant technological advancements of the 21st century. The ability to collect, process, and analyze vast amounts of data in real-time has revolutionized decision-making in many industries, including healthcare, finance, transportation, and manufacturing, among others. However, despite the numerous benefits of big data and streaming data, cataloging this data to make it easily accessible, discoverable, and usable presents considerable challenges.

The concept of data cataloging entails organizing data to allow easy retrieval, comprehension, and management. It entails collecting metadata and information about various data assets within an organization. This approach allows end-users, such as data scientists, data analysts, and other decision-makers, to quickly discover and use the data resources to generate insights.

Challenges of cataloging big data

When it comes to big data, data cataloging becomes a herculean task due to the following challenges:

Volume and variety of data

One of the defining features of big data is its volume. Organizations now have access to petabytes or even exabytes of data, which they can analyze to gain critical business insights. This data comes in a variety of forms, including structured, unstructured, and semi-structured data, sourced from different locations like databases, cloud-based applications, IoT devices, social media, and more. Cataloging such a diverse and massive dataset is inherently complex. It requires robust tools and strategies that can scale according to the data's volume and handle different types of data formats.

Data ingestion and integration

The nature of big data implies that data is continually flowing into the organization's systems. In this real-time environment, cataloging should occur concurrently with data ingestion. This need for real-time or near-real-time cataloging poses significant challenges, particularly regarding integration. As data from various sources and in different formats is ingested, it must be integrated and cataloged to maintain its accessibility and usefulness.

Data quality and consistency

Maintaining the quality and consistency of big data is another significant challenge. Given the wide variety of sources from which data is derived, ensuring that the data is accurate, reliable, and consistent can be difficult. Poor quality data can lead to misleading analyses and erroneous decisions. Therefore, a crucial part of the data cataloging process involves data cleaning and transformation to ensure that the data meets the required quality standards.

Metadata management

Metadata, or data about the data, plays a critical role in cataloging. It describes the data's origin, structure, and meaning, among other things. In big data contexts, metadata management becomes an uphill task due to the sheer volume of data. With each new piece of data ingested, more metadata gets created, and managing this metadata to ensure it stays relevant and accurate becomes a significant challenge.

Data governance and compliance

With the advent of various data protection regulations such as GDPR, CCPA, and HIPAA, among others, organizations are now required to ensure the security and privacy of the data they handle. Data cataloging should thus be done in a way that facilitates data governance and ensures compliance with these regulations. This task entails tracking the lineage of data, controlling who has access to what data, auditing data usage, and so forth. Implementing these measures in a big data environment presents a considerable challenge due to the complex and dynamic nature of such ecosystems.

User accessibility

A fundamental purpose of data cataloging is to make data easily discoverable and accessible for end-users. However, big data's complexity can render this objective challenging to achieve. Designing a user-friendly interface that enables users to effortlessly discover and use data, despite the underlying complexity of the data environment, is a challenge that must be addressed during the cataloging process.

Resource and infrastructure constraints

Last but not least, cataloging big data often requires significant computational resources and advanced infrastructure. The necessary processing power, storage capacity, and advanced software tools can be beyond the reach of some organizations, especially small and medium-sized enterprises. These resource constraints can limit the efficiency and effectiveness of data cataloging efforts.

Although cataloging big data presents numerous challenges, it is a necessary undertaking for organizations seeking to harness the full potential of their data. Addressing these challenges requires a combination of advanced technology, comprehensive strategies, and skilled human resources. The development of more sophisticated data cataloging tools, together with ongoing research into data management best practices, will go a long way in mitigating these challenges. Despite the complexity involved, the rewards of successful data cataloging – improved decision-making, increased operational efficiency, and enhanced competitive advantage – are well worth the effort.

Cataloging data from streaming sources

In the era of big data, cataloging and managing data in real-time has become a significant challenge. The evolution of big data has seen a shift from batch processing to real-time data streaming, making data cataloging an essential yet complex task. This section aims to provide an in-depth perspective on cataloging data from streaming sources, considering the new opportunities and challenges presented by big data and streaming data.

Understanding streaming data

Streaming data is data that is generated continuously by various sources. This data can be ingested in real or near-real-time. Streaming data includes a wide variety of data, such as log files generated by customer interactions on websites, social media feeds, IoT device data, and live transactional data, among others.

One of the critical characteristics of streaming data is its high velocity. Streaming data is produced swiftly and continuously, making it a valuable source for real-time analytics and decision-making processes.

Data cataloging plays a critical role in managing big data. It aids in organizing vast amounts of data, making it easier for data analysts and scientists to find the needed data and understand it better.

Cataloging data from streaming sources involves recording metadata about the data stream, such as the source of the data, the format, and the date and time the data was received, among other information. Metadata provides context for the data, allowing users to understand the data better and derive meaningful insights from the data.

Challenges in cataloging streaming data

The process of cataloging streaming data is not without its challenges. First, the volume of streaming data can be overwhelming, and cataloging such massive amounts of data can be computationally expensive. Without appropriate techniques and tools, this can lead to performance degradation and increased latency in data processing.

Second, the velocity of streaming data poses a challenge. Traditional data cataloging techniques may not be able to keep pace with the rapid inflow of streaming data, resulting in a delay in cataloging and potential data loss.

Third, the variety of streaming data makes cataloging complex. With data coming in from multiple sources in different formats, cataloging needs to be adaptable to handle this diversity. Ensuring data cataloging can cope with both structured and unstructured data is crucial.

Strategies for effective streaming data cataloging include:

- **Real-time cataloging**. Traditional cataloging methods, which were designed for batch processing of data, might not be practical for streaming data. To address the high velocity of streaming data, cataloging must happen in real-time or near-real-time. Implementing real-time cataloging can involve using technologies like Apache Kafka or Amazon Kinesis to handle the speed and volume of incoming data.

- **Automated metadata generation**. Automation is a vital strategy in managing the high volume of streaming data. By automating the creation of metadata, organizations can ensure that all incoming data is cataloged without manual intervention, reducing the likelihood of errors and improving efficiency. ML and AI technologies can play a role here in predicting metadata for incoming data.

- **Standardization of formats**. Due to the variety of data formats, having a standard format can simplify the cataloging process. This might involve transforming incoming data into a consistent format before cataloging, using tools such as data pipelines and ETL processes.

- **Decentralized cataloging**. Considering the high volume of streaming data, a centralized cataloging system might not be sustainable. A decentralized approach, where each data source is responsible for cataloging its data, can distribute the load and increase the system's overall efficiency.

- **Effective data governance**. Ensuring data accuracy and security is another challenge in cataloging streaming data. Establishing strong data governance rules is essential to maintain data integrity, prevent data breaches, and ensure compliance with data privacy regulations.

- **Scalable systems**. Given the growth rate of data, systems used for cataloging must be scalable. They should be able to handle an increase in data volume without significant degradation in performance. Cloud-based cataloging systems can be a solution here, as they provide elasticity and can be scaled up or down based on demand.

Cataloging data from streaming sources is a complex but necessary part of managing big data. The high volume, velocity, and variety of streaming data necessitate innovative strategies and technologies to ensure efficient and effective cataloging. While challenges exist, advancements in ML, AI, and cloud technologies pave the way for more effective data cataloging solutions. By implementing robust and scalable cataloging systems, organizations can harness the full potential of streaming data, driving real-time insights and facilitating informed decision-making.

Real-time data cataloging solutions

The surge in data generation, coupled with its velocity, variety, and veracity, has caused the development of new strategies for managing and cataloging data. In this context, real-time data cataloging solutions have become an indispensable part of the data lifecycle, aiming to maintain data inventory, manage metadata, ensure data quality, and facilitate efficient data discovery and access.

A data catalog is an organized inventory of data assets in an organization. Traditional data cataloging involves collecting and storing metadata that helps describe, locate, and understand the data. However, as the data landscape evolves to incorporate real-time streaming data, the cataloging process also requires real-time solutions.

Real-time data cataloging involves the immediate cataloging and indexing of data as it streams into the data infrastructure. It is about ensuring that metadata gets updated the moment a change occurs in the data landscape – a new data set gets added, an existing one gets modified, or a data stream changes its structure or content. This capability provides a huge advantage in managing real-time or near-real-time data streams that require immediate analysis or that form the basis of time-sensitive decision-making processes.

Big data refers to datasets whose size, speed, or variety exceeds the ability of typical database software tools to capture, manage, and process within an acceptable timeframe. In many cases, Big Data involves streaming data, which are generated continuously by different sources. Typical sources of streaming data include log files, sensors, IoT devices, social media feeds, and more.

Real-time cataloging becomes especially critical for big data and streaming data for several reasons:

- **Accelerated data discovery**. Big data environments often consist of vast amounts of data spread across different systems and formats. Real-time cataloging accelerates data discovery by ensuring that it is cataloged and indexed as soon as data enters the system. This enables analysts and data scientists to instantly access fresh data for timely insights.

- **Enhanced data governance**. Real-time cataloging promotes better data governance. It helps to maintain an updated view of the data landscape, which is necessary for data protection and privacy compliance. When data elements are tagged in real-time, it becomes much easier to enforce security controls and comply with regulations like GDPR and CCPA.

- **Improved data quality**. The faster you catalog data, the quicker you can implement data quality controls. Real-time cataloging allows organizations to spot and correct errors or inconsistencies as soon as the data enters the system, improving overall data quality.

- **Facilitated real-time analytics.** Real-time cataloging facilitates real-time analytics and decision-making. As data is cataloged in real-time, analytics tools can access and analyze the data almost immediately, leading to faster insights and quicker actions.

Real-time data cataloging solutions have a range of features that allow them to perform their role effectively:

- **Real-time metadata collection.** This is the core feature of real-time data cataloging solutions. These solutions continuously scan data sources to collect and update metadata as soon as changes occur. This capability is vital in environments where data is continuously changing or updating, like streaming data.

- **Scalability.** Given the volume and velocity of Big Data and streaming data, real-time cataloging solutions must be scalable. They should be able to handle increasing amounts of data without compromising performance.

- **Data lineage.** Data lineage refers to the life cycle of data, including its origins, movements, transformations, and interactions. Real-time data cataloging solutions track data lineage in real-time, which aids in data governance, quality control, and compliance.

- **Search and discovery**. Real-time data cataloging solutions provide advanced search and discovery features. This includes full-text search, faceted search, and NLP capabilities that make it easy to locate and access data.

- **Integration capabilities**. These solutions should be able to integrate seamlessly with different data sources, data management tools, and data analytics platforms. This ensures that the data catalog is always synchronized with the rest of the data ecosystem.

Real-time data cataloging in practice

Several solutions exist in the market that offer real-time data cataloging capabilities. Alation, Collibra, and Informatica's Enterprise Data Catalog are among the leading providers. They provide a unified, real-time view of data across various sources, making it easier for businesses to find, understand, and govern their data.

For instance, Alation uses ML to catalog data and update metadata in real-time automatically. It offers a Google-like search interface for easy data discovery. Similarly, Collibra

Catalog is a single source of intelligence for data experts and users, offering automated data lineage, extensive integrations, and a user-friendly interface for data discovery.

Moreover, open-source solutions like Apache Atlas provide real-time data cataloging for big data platforms. Apache Atlas offers scalable governance for Enterprise Hadoop that includes metadata and data lineage features.

As organizations continue to grapple with Big Data and streaming data, real-time data cataloging solutions will play an increasingly vital role in effective data management. These solutions not only streamline data discovery but also enhance data governance and facilitate real-time analytics. By adopting a robust real-time data cataloging solution, organizations can ensure they are well-equipped to leverage their data assets for strategic decision-making and insights.

Key learnings

Cataloging big data introduces complexities such as managing volume and variety, ensuring real-time ingestion, maintaining quality, handling metadata, and adhering to governance regulations, all while ensuring user accessibility and managing resources.

Streaming data cataloging presents its own challenges, notably managing its constant, high-velocity flow, diverse data types, and ensuring ongoing accuracy and security.

Implementing effective strategies for streaming data, such as real-time cataloging, automated metadata generation, and scalable systems, is crucial to manage its unique challenges.

Real-time data cataloging enhances data discovery, governance, and quality, while also facilitating real-time analytics, emphasizing its importance in managing streaming data.

Key features of real-time cataloging solutions encompass immediate metadata collection, scalability, data lineage tracking, advanced search capabilities, and compatibility with various data sources.

PART V

Utilizing the Data Catalog

CHAPTER 12

Data Catalog for Data Consumers

A data catalog can be conceptualized as a systematic and methodical inventory of data assets. It is often likened to a library's card catalog, providing a snapshot of what data exists, where it resides, and how it can be accessed. This digital inventory is replete with metadata, data profiles, and data lineage information that enable users to understand the data landscape in their organization.

How data consumers benefit from catalogs

Data consumers refer to a broad audience, including data scientists, business analysts, data engineers, decision-makers, and any other individual or entity that utilizes data. Now, let's understand how data catalogs benefit these consumers.

Enhancing data discovery

Without a data catalog, finding the correct data for analysis or decision-making can be akin to searching for a needle in a haystack. A data catalog improves data discovery by offering a central repository where data consumers can quickly search and locate data assets. By using metadata and advanced search functionalities, data consumers can identify relevant datasets based on attributes such as data source, data type, and other specific characteristics.

Facilitating data understanding

Data catalogs don't just tell you where the data is; they also provide valuable insights about the data. By capturing and presenting metadata, a data catalog can provide information about a dataset's origin, transformations it has undergone, relations with other data, and more. Some advanced data catalogs also incorporate ML to suggest correlations and patterns, enabling data consumers to understand the data better before diving into analysis.

Improving data quality

Data catalogs often include features for assessing and scoring data quality, ensuring that data consumers don't waste their time on irrelevant or poor-quality data. By integrating with data quality tools, data catalogs can provide insight into data health, such as accuracy, completeness, consistency, and timeliness. High-quality data not only leads to more accurate analysis but also improves confidence in decision-making.

Enabling data governance and compliance

Data catalogs can be instrumental in enforcing data governance policies and facilitating regulatory compliance. By cataloging data assets and capturing metadata, they provide a transparent view of what data is collected, how it's used, and who has access. Data lineage features further enable the traceability of data, an essential aspect for compliance with regulations like GDPR or CCPA.

Fostering collaboration and knowledge sharing

Data catalogs can also play a role in fostering collaboration among data consumers. A data catalog can become a knowledge repository by providing a platform where users can annotate data, share insights, and validate each other's findings. This collaboration can shorten the learning curve for new data consumers and reduce the duplication of efforts, leading to increased productivity.

Increasing data literacy

With a data catalog, the mystery surrounding data is diminished, leading to increased data literacy across the organization. By providing an accessible and user-friendly interface, data catalogs can empower non-technical users to interact with data more confidently. As more people start using data in their roles, organizations can become more data-driven.

Promoting data democratization

By providing a central point of access, data catalogs can democratize data, allowing more people in the organization to locate and understand data. This democratization breaks down data silos and enables a more inclusive data culture.

Enhancing analytical efficiency

Data catalogs can also speed up analytical workflows. By saving data consumers the time spent searching for data or trying to understand unfamiliar datasets, they can focus more on data analysis. This efficiency not only accelerates the time-to-insight but also leads to more robust analysis.

A data catalog offers manifold benefits to data consumers. By enhancing data discovery, facilitating data understanding, improving data quality, enabling data governance and compliance, fostering collaboration and knowledge sharing, increasing data literacy, promoting data democratization, and enhancing analytical efficiency, it becomes an indispensable tool in the data-driven organization's arsenal. As we continue to navigate the ever-growing data landscape, the role of data catalogs will only become more vital in empowering data consumers to leverage data effectively and efficiently.

Navigating and searching the data catalog

As the importance of data analytics in decision-making continues to grow, effectively utilizing a data catalog has become a crucial skill for data consumers. Data catalogs serve as repositories of information about an organization's data assets. They help users understand the data's source, its associations, and its usage. This section focuses on the critical aspects of navigating and searching within a data catalog.

Understanding the data catalog structure

The foundation of effective data catalog usage lies in understanding its structure. This typically comprises metadata—data that provides insightful information about other data. It contains details about the data's origin, purpose, interconnections, and prior usage. Typical components of a data catalog include:

- **Datasets**. Datasets are essentially data collections in various formats, such as tables, files, or API endpoints. Each dataset comes with a summary, owner details, the date it was last updated, and other relevant information.

- **Schema**. A schema outlines the organization of data within a dataset. It can encompass information about data types, field descriptions, and relationships with other datasets.

- **Tags/labels**. Tags or labels are keywords associated with datasets to enhance their searchability. They could indicate the dataset's content, intended use case, or other categorical information.

- **Data lineage**. Data lineage is a roadmap of the data's lifecycle, outlining its origin, journey, and transformation.

- **Usage metrics**. These parameters highlight how frequently a dataset is used and by whom. They are instrumental in identifying critical datasets within an organization.

- **Data quality metrics**. These metrics offer insights into the quality and reliability of the data.

Strategies for navigating the data catalog

Navigating a data catalog can occur at varying levels of granularity, from a high-level overview to an in-depth metadata inspection:

- **Exploring at a high level**. Begin by grasping the catalog's overall organization. Understanding how the catalog is divided at the top level (such as by business unit, data source, or data type) can provide a sense of what's available.

- **Drilling down into specific areas**. Once you have a feel for the high-level structure, delve into specific areas. For instance, explore datasets associated with a particular business unit or those originating from a specific source.

- **Inspecting individual datasets**. After narrowing your focus to a specific area, proceed to inspect individual datasets. This involves examining the dataset summary, reviewing its schema, perusing its data lineage, and more.

Effective searching within a data catalog is another critical skill. Here are several strategies to conduct robust searches:

- **Keyword searches**. Start with a general keyword search. Use the search bar to input a keyword related to the data you are seeking. If the catalog uses tagging, these keywords could match with tags, dataset names, descriptions, or any other text associated with the datasets.

- **Filtering.** After conducting a keyword search, it's likely you will need to narrow down the results. Most data catalogs offer various filtering options, such as by data source, data type, owner, last updated, and more. Using these filters appropriately can expedite your search for the most relevant datasets.

- **Sorting.** Many data catalogs also allow you to sort the search results. This is particularly helpful when you are looking for the most recent data or the most utilized data.

Many data catalogs incorporate advanced search options. These include Boolean searches (using keywords combined with operators like AND, NOT, and OR), phrase searches (searching for exact phrases), proximity searches (searching for two or more words that occur within a certain number of words from each other), and wildcard searches (using symbols to represent unknown words or parts of words).

Comprehending data lineage and quality metrics is crucial for data consumers. Data lineage allows users to trace data from its original source to its current state, assuring its reliability and veracity. Users can monitor all transformations the data has undergone, improving their understanding and trust in the data.

Data quality metrics, on the other hand, provide a direct indication of the dataset's quality. These metrics include completeness (the extent to which data is populated), uniqueness (whether the data contains duplicate entries), timeliness (how up-to-date the data is), and accuracy (how accurately the data reflects the real world). Using high-quality data results in more accurate analyses and, consequently, more informed decisions.

Effectively navigating and searching a data catalog involves a solid understanding of its structure and various search strategies. When you can deftly maneuver these tools, you significantly enhance your ability to find the correct data swiftly and confidently, leading to more valuable insights and better decision-making processes.

Requesting and accessing data

A data catalog offers a centralized view of an organization's data, irrespective of where that data is physically stored. It captures metadata including, but not limited to, data source, data type, data lineage, data quality, business definitions, and related attributes. It offers a robust search function to allow data consumers to discover and understand the data. Furthermore, it maintains the data's context, relationships, and lineage, which can provide essential insight into how data is captured, transformed, and utilized throughout the organization.

However, the simple existence of a data catalog doesn't automatically ensure optimal data consumption. The key lies in understanding how to navigate, request, and access data within the catalog to extract meaningful insights effectively.

A data catalog should provide a user-friendly interface for navigating the various data assets. The search function is central to this. By using specific keywords or filters such as data sources, data types, or other metadata tags, users can quickly locate the relevant data sets.

Once the search results are available, data consumers can delve deeper into individual data assets. A detailed view would typically include a wealth of metadata, such as the data's business description, its format and type, data quality measures, its source and lineage, and so on. All this information is crucial in understanding the data and its relevance to your specific use case.

Requesting data

Once the relevant data sets have been identified, the next step is to request access to the data. The process of doing this varies between organizations and their specific governance policies. Some data catalogs might provide an automated request process, while others might involve raising a formal request to a data steward or data owner.

When requesting data, it's essential to articulate the purpose for which the data will be used clearly. This includes the context of the project, the specific insights or questions you aim to address, and how the data will be handled and stored. Some data catalogs might have a built-in feature to enter this information as a part of the request process. This transparency is essential not only for ethical data usage but also to ensure compliance with data privacy regulations.

Accessing data

Once your data request has been approved, the next step is to access the data. The specifics of this process again depend on the organization's data architecture and governance policies. Some data catalogs might provide direct data access within the tool, while others might require the use of external data analysis tools.

When accessing the data, it's crucial to keep data security and privacy considerations in mind. This includes using secure methods to access the data, ensuring appropriate data masking or anonymization where necessary, and not sharing data inappropriately.

In some cases, instead of providing direct access to the actual data, the data catalog might provide a "data view." A data view is a representation of the data that allows users to perform analysis without actually handling the raw data. This can be particularly useful when dealing with sensitive data, where direct access might not be permissible.

It's also worth noting that some data catalogs offer "sandbox" environments. These are isolated computing environments where data consumers can freely explore and manipulate data without affecting the original data sets or other users. These environments can be advantageous when testing hypotheses or performing exploratory data analysis.

The importance of data lineage

Finally, let's touch upon data lineage – a critical aspect of metadata that is closely tied to requesting and accessing data. Data lineage refers to the data's life cycle, tracking its origin, movements, transformations, and consumption.

Understanding data lineage is crucial for several reasons. Firstly, it offers insights into the data's quality and reliability. If you can trace the data back to its original source and understand all the transformations it has undergone, you can have greater confidence in its accuracy. Secondly, it provides context. Knowing how data is used and transformed throughout the organization can help you understand it better and use it more effectively. Finally, understanding data lineage is crucial for regulatory compliance, especially for regulations requiring data traceability.

As a data consumer, knowing how to request and access data from a data catalog can significantly streamline your data discovery and consumption process. Understanding how to navigate the catalog, the process for requesting data, how to access it securely, and the importance of data lineage, can help you harness the power of your organization's data more effectively. The data catalog is not just a directory of data assets but a tool that when used effectively, can lead to richer insights and more intelligent decision-making.

Key learnings

A data catalog systematically inventories data assets, providing metadata, data profiles, and lineage to enhance data discovery and understanding.

Comprehending a data catalog's structure, including datasets, schema, tags, lineage, and usage and quality metrics, is pivotal.

Effectively navigating a data catalog entails strategies like high-level exploration, specific area drilling, and individual dataset inspection.

Understanding data lineage and quality metrics is crucial for tracing data's journey and assessing its quality.

Navigating and accessing data within a catalog necessitates knowledge of its structure, clarity in data request purpose, and the use of secure access methods, with a keen consideration for data security, privacy, and lineage understanding.

CHAPTER 13

Data Catalog for Data Governance and Compliance

Effective data governance and compliance have become integral for modern businesses, and a data catalog plays a central role in ensuring these. Organizations are not just dealing with ever-increasing data volumes but also navigating a complex web of data compliance and regulatory requirements. The importance of data compliance cannot be overstated, as failure to meet these requirements can lead to hefty penalties, reputational damage, and potential business losses.

The role of a data catalog in data compliance

Data compliance refers to the management of data in line with a relevant regulatory framework. This framework may be a law, an industry-specific regulation, or a set of guidelines provided by a regulator. Compliance involves ensuring data security, privacy, integrity, and availability, among other things, are following these prescribed rules. This is where the data catalog, a centralized repository for storing metadata, comes in handy. It provides a robust foundation for data governance and compliance.

Centralizing metadata for compliance

Data catalogs offer an organized view of enterprise data assets, creating a single source of truth that helps streamline data governance and compliance efforts. By centralizing metadata and providing comprehensive visibility into an organization's data ecosystem, data catalogs enable businesses to adhere to a broad spectrum of regulations, including GDPR, CCPA, HIPAA, and others.

The cornerstone of any effective data compliance strategy is understanding what data you have and where it resides. A data catalog, with its metadata management capability, provides an overview of the existing data, its location, the processes it goes through, its lineage, and the people responsible for it. This is particularly critical when dealing with sensitive data, such as PII, PHI, and financial data, which are often subject to strict compliance requirements.

Leveraging data lineage for regulatory requirements

Data catalogs facilitate better data visibility and traceability. This is done by tracing data lineage, which allows organizations to identify where data originated, how it was transformed, and where it currently resides. Traceability is a critical compliance feature, especially for financial and health sectors, where auditors require detailed records of how data has been used and modified.

Managing data privacy and confidentiality

Data catalogs can also be invaluable for managing data privacy and confidentiality. They can be used to implement RBAC (Role-Based Access Control), where users are only permitted to access data for which they have been granted permissions. This way, sensitive data can be shielded from unauthorized access, ensuring compliance with regulations like HIPAA, which stipulates stringent safeguards to protect patient data.

Enhancing data classification

Moreover, data catalogs aid in data classification. They categorize data based on their sensitivity level, relevance, and usability. Classifying data according to its sensitivity (e.g., public, internal, confidential, or restricted) ensures that strict security measures are applied to more sensitive data types, thereby achieving compliance with data protection laws.

Integrating AI and ML

The integration of AI and ML with data catalogs has brought a new level of capability in data compliance. AI/ML-powered data catalogs can automatically discover sensitive data and apply appropriate classifications. They can also suggest data protection measures based on the type and sensitivity of data. This proactive approach to data compliance is a quantum leap from the traditional reactive methods.

Data catalogs within a data governance framework

However, while data catalogs can significantly enhance data compliance, they are not a standalone solution. They should be part of a comprehensive data governance strategy that includes data quality management, data privacy management, and an established data culture that values compliance and ethical data usage.

With the continuously evolving data regulatory landscape, it has become essential for organizations to leverage tools like data catalogs that can help navigate the complex world of data compliance. Not only do data catalogs provide a holistic view of the enterprise's data ecosystem, but they also facilitate compliance with regulations, enhance data privacy and protection, and foster a culture of transparency and trust.

By integrating the data catalog into their data governance strategy, organizations can turn regulatory compliance from a cumbersome obligation into a competitive advantage. It can lead to improved customer trust, operational efficiency, and, ultimately, business success. After all, in today's data-driven world, good data governance is good business.

Auditing and monitoring data usage

A key element in effectively implementing a data governance strategy, such as using a data catalog, is understanding, monitoring, and auditing data usage. These processes ensure that the data catalog is employed correctly and data compliance rules are adhered to, providing data protection and data privacy.

Before diving into auditing and monitoring, let's briefly discuss understanding data usage. This refers to knowing how data moves through your organization, who uses it, for what purposes, and how often it's accessed. This understanding is pivotal in achieving a solid data governance framework and allows for effective auditing and monitoring processes.

A data catalog aids this process by documenting data assets, where they originate, their transformations, and their purpose. It provides the ability to trace data lineage, enabling organizations to understand where data comes from, how it moves, and how it changes, a process crucial for effective auditing and monitoring.

Monitoring data usage

Monitoring data usage involves continuously tracking and reviewing how data is accessed and used across the organization. This ongoing process is vital in recognizing and responding to potential data misuse or breaches in real-time.

The data catalog serves as an essential tool for monitoring. It offers a unified view of all data assets, making it easier to observe any anomalies in data access or use. Furthermore, modern data catalogs come with automated monitoring features. These tools can raise alerts in case of unusual data access patterns or when sensitive data is accessed by unauthorized users.

For example, suppose an employee not working in the financial department suddenly starts accessing sensitive financial data. In that case, an alert can be triggered, allowing the data governance team to investigate and take appropriate actions if necessary.

Auditing data usage

While monitoring is a real-time activity, auditing data usage is a more comprehensive, periodic review of data access and usage patterns. It's aimed at assessing whether data policies and compliance standards are being adhered to and identifying potential areas of improvement.

The data catalog can play a pivotal role in auditing. First, it makes data assets more discoverable, enabling auditors to find the necessary data quickly. Second, maintaining metadata and data lineage provides auditors with context, helping them understand the data's origins, transformations, and relationships.

Moreover, a data catalog may track a history of data usage, including who has accessed what data, when, and for what purpose. This audit trail is essential for demonstrating compliance with data protection regulations like GDPR and CCPA, which require organizations to show where personal data is stored and who has access to it.

In this way, the data catalog not only simplifies auditing processes but also enhances their accuracy and effectiveness. Auditing data usage through a data catalog can reveal critical insights, like the frequency of data access, the users who access the data most often, and potential misuse or non-compliance incidents.

Auditing and monitoring for compliance

Given the increasing rigor of data protection laws worldwide, ensuring compliance is a non-negotiable part of data governance. Both auditing and monitoring are instrumental in achieving and maintaining compliance.

Organizations can tag sensitive data with a data catalog to indicate they are subject to specific regulations. Doing so makes the monitoring and auditing processes more efficient and effective as they can quickly identify which data sets require extra care treatment. In the case of a compliance audit, having this information readily available can significantly expedite the process.

Moreover, robust data catalogs also facilitate "right to be forgotten" requests under laws like the GDPR. By maintaining a complete data lineage and data usage history, they allow organizations to locate and remove an individual's data across all storage locations, a process that would be incredibly complex without such a tool.

Auditing and monitoring are pivotal to data governance and compliance. A data catalog provides a robust platform to make these processes more efficient and effective, offering metadata management, data lineage, and data usage tracking features. It enables organizations to have a comprehensive view of their data, ensuring that their data usage aligns with their policies and compliance requirements.

As the landscape of data regulations becomes more complex, the need for practical data governance tools, such as a data catalog, becomes ever more critical. To not only keep up with but also stay ahead of these changes, businesses must adopt a proactive approach to their data governance strategy.

By leveraging a data catalog for auditing and monitoring, organizations can gain complete visibility into their data landscape, safeguard their sensitive information, and ensure they meet their compliance obligations, thus enabling them to use their data confidently and effectively.

Data catalogs in data privacy initiatives

As our global society transitions into a data-driven ecosystem, data privacy and protection have emerged as critical elements in data governance. The drive towards realizing the full potential of data and analytics is catalyzed by the growing realization that data is indeed the new oil. However, as data collection, storage, and analysis continue to accelerate, so do the concerns about the misuse, misinterpretation, or unauthorized access to this valuable resource. This underpins the increased focus on data privacy initiatives and the need for comprehensive data governance.

The data catalog is instrumental in these data governance and privacy initiatives. A data catalog serves as a comprehensive inventory of data assets within an organization, replete with information about what data exists, where it's located, and what its attributes are. It is designed to help users find and understand the data, thus improving the quality of analytics and decision-making. Moreover, when properly utilized, a data catalog can significantly contribute to data privacy initiatives and compliance, forming the backbone of a sound data governance framework.

Firstly, by consolidating metadata and providing clear visibility into all data assets, data catalogs can ensure better data control. They map out data landscapes, making it possible to track where sensitive or PII is stored. This ability to trace and monitor PII is crucial in the era of stringent data protection regulations like the GDPR and the CCPA. With a robust data catalog, organizations can demonstrate compliance with data protection laws by showing where all instances of a particular type of data reside.

Secondly, data catalogs often come equipped with data lineage capabilities, allowing organizations to follow the lifecycle of their data. They provide insights into where data originates, how it's transformed and used, and where it's disseminated. Such visibility is vital for conducting privacy impact assessments and audits, and it helps data stewards ensure that all transformations and usage are in line with privacy rules.

In addition, a well-structured data catalog can facilitate data anonymization, pseudonymization, and tokenization procedures. For instance, once sensitive data assets are identified within the catalog, they can be anonymized to protect the privacy of individuals involved, reducing the risk of data breaches. This proactive approach not only ensures the organization's compliance with data privacy laws but also fosters trust among customers and partners.

Data catalogs can also help enforce data minimization principles. Data minimization involves collecting only the necessary data and retaining it only for the required duration, a concept heavily advocated in privacy-focused regulations like GDPR. By providing a clear map of what data is collected and how long it is stored, data catalogs can help organizations ensure they aren't retaining more data than needed or for longer than necessary, avoiding potential regulatory pitfalls.

Moreover, data catalogs can support the implementation of privacy by design and, by default, two fundamental principles of data protection regulation. Privacy by design ensures that privacy is incorporated into systems and processes during their design phase, while privacy by default guarantees that the strictest privacy settings apply by default without any manual input from the end user.

Data catalogs can help organizations apply these principles by providing clear visibility into all data processes, enabling the design and implementation of privacy-conscious systems.

The effective utilization of data catalogs

While data catalogs can prove highly beneficial for data privacy initiatives, their effectiveness is dependent on several factors. For instance, data catalogs need to be regularly updated to reflect the changing data landscape of the organization. If they aren't up-to-date, they can provide a false sense of security about data privacy compliance. Similarly, the metadata quality within the catalog is a crucial determinant of its utility. If metadata is poorly maintained or inaccurate, the catalog's usefulness for privacy initiatives may be compromised.

In addition, we cannot ignore the human element. While data catalogs can provide the necessary tools and resources for data privacy, the organization's data culture will determine how effectively these tools are used. The entire organization, from top executives to front-line staff, must be engaged in data privacy initiatives for them to succeed.

Data catalogs play a critical role in data privacy initiatives, forming an integral part of any robust data governance framework. By consolidating metadata, providing data lineage, facilitating data anonymization, enforcing data minimization principles, and supporting privacy by design and by default, data catalogs can help organizations navigate the complex terrain of data privacy laws and regulations. However, their effectiveness is dependent on regular updates, high-quality metadata, and a robust data culture within the organization. With these elements in place, data catalogs can be a powerful ally in the quest for data privacy and compliance.

Key learnings

Data catalogs boost visibility and traceability in compliance, offering insights into data location, transformations, and custodianship by tracing data lineage.

The integration of AI and ML with data catalogs has innovated data compliance by automating the discovery and classification of sensitive data.

Data catalogs should be embedded within a holistic data governance strategy, as they are not standalone solutions for data compliance.

By turning regulatory compliance into a competitive edge, data catalogs can enhance transparency, trust, operational efficiency, and business prosperity.

Implementing a data governance strategy using a data catalog necessitates understanding, monitoring, and auditing data usage, with catalogs enabling data lineage tracing and thorough auditing.

Data catalogs serve as the backbone of solid data governance, enhancing data control, facilitating data anonymization, enforcing data minimization, and supporting privacy by design and default.

CHAPTER 14

Data Catalog for Business Intelligence

Data discovery has become a pivotal part of the modern business world, primarily due to the ceaseless generation and consumption of data. In an age where data is not just an asset but an omnipresent entity, it significantly impacts decision-making, forms the crux of strategies, and acts as a catalyst for innovation.

Data discovery refers to the process of identifying patterns, anomalies, correlations, and trends within data sources. It uses a wide range of technologies to extract actionable insights from data, enabling users to generate business-related queries and build an intuitive understanding of the data. The process encompasses several vital steps, including data collection, data cleaning, data integration, and the application of analytics tools and visualization techniques.

Given the colossal volumes of data modern businesses generate, traditional data discovery methods often fall short. Here, a robust and well-implemented data catalog becomes an indispensable tool. It helps manage and harness the potential of big data, enabling organizations to unearth deep, data-driven insights.

A data catalog is a structured set of metadata housing information about datasets, databases, and various other data assets within an organization. Essentially, it is an inventory of available data that provides a holistic view of all data assets. By making it simpler to locate and understand the relevant data needed for analysis, a data catalog significantly enhances the efficiency and effectiveness of the data discovery process.

Unlocking business analytics with data catalogs

There are several distinct advantages of employing a data catalog in data discovery, all of which benefit business analytics and intelligence:

- **Accessibility and democratization of data**. A data catalog makes data more accessible to a diverse range of users across an organization. It enables non-technical users to identify data sources and understand their contents without needing big data engineering expertise. This democratization of data access empowers users to perform self-service analytics, thus promoting an organization-wide data-driven culture.

- **Enhanced understanding of data.** A data catalog enriches metadata with a business context, providing more depth to the data. This could include information about data lineage (such as its source, history, and usage), relationships between datasets, or business glossaries defining business terms and key performance indicators (KPIs). This enrichment not only enhances users' understanding of data but also allows for more accurate and relevant insights to be derived.

- **Efficient data governance.** Effective data governance is another advantage of a well-maintained data catalog. By documenting the lineage and lifecycle of data assets, a data catalog assists in managing data privacy, ensuring compliance with data regulations, and maintaining data quality.

- **Accelerated data discovery.** A data catalog enables users to navigate the vast data landscape of an organization quickly and efficiently. Through keyword search functionality, users can swiftly find the datasets they need. Some advanced data catalogs employ ML algorithms to provide recommendations based on user behavior, further enhancing the speed and efficiency of data discovery.

- **Promoting data collaboration**. A data catalog encourages data collaboration by providing a platform where users can share findings, comment on datasets, and exchange knowledge about data usage. This collaborative environment fosters a data-centric culture where insights and knowledge are freely shared, leading to more comprehensive and accurate analyses.

The impact of data culture transformation

It is critical to understand that implementing a data catalog is more than just incorporating a new tool; it signifies a transformative shift in an organization's data culture. Organizations need to nurture an environment where data is not just recognized as an asset but is effectively utilized for decision-making. To ensure this, employees must be trained and supported to familiarize themselves with the data catalog tool, encouraging its use in data discovery.

An organization's ability to extract valuable insights from its data largely hinges on the efficiency of its data discovery process. A well-implemented data catalog can substantially augment this process by improving data accessibility, understanding, governance, discovery speed, and collaboration.

A data catalog is a powerful enabler for data analytics and BI. It aids in organizing and understanding data, empowers users to unearth meaningful insights, and drives informed business decisions. The potent combination of a data catalog and data discovery will undoubtedly continue to play a pivotal role in the future data-driven landscape. Thus, organizations must proactively adopt and harness these tools and techniques to stay competitive in the era of big data and analytics.

Enhancing data analytics with the data catalog

One of the significant hurdles data scientists, analysts, and other data professionals face is not just having data but accessing the correct data at the right time. A data catalog, an organized inventory of data assets in an organization, can streamline this process by enhancing data discoverability, accessibility, and comprehension. Here's an in-depth look at how a data catalog can optimize data analytics workflows and drive informed decision-making processes in the realm of BI.

The data catalog provides a holistic view of all available data assets in a searchable and organized manner. Data catalogs use metadata, often coupled with ML algorithms, to create rich context around each data asset. They provide detailed information such as data origin, transformations, relationships, quality, usage, and much more, rendering data comprehension easier.

Data discoverability

The first step in any data analytics process is identifying the data sources relevant to the task. This step is increasingly challenging with the exponential increase in data volumes and variety, especially without an effective mechanism to locate the required data. This is where a data catalog can be a game-changer.

A data catalog acts as a single source of truth for all data assets within an organization. By centralizing metadata and offering search capabilities akin to a web search engine, a data catalog drastically enhances data discoverability. For instance, analysts can use specific keywords to locate datasets relevant to their analytics tasks quickly, saving precious time and resources.

Data understanding

Understanding the context of data is crucial for accurate and reliable analytics. A data catalog significantly enhances this understanding through comprehensive metadata management. This metadata can include administrative technical metadata (data types, volume, etc.), structural metadata (data origin, transformations, etc.), and descriptive metadata (business definitions, ownership, etc.).

This breadth of information aids in understanding the applicability and relevance of the data to the analytics task. Moreover, the data lineage provided by the data catalog provides a clear view of the data's lifecycle, improving transparency and trust in data.

Data quality insights

The data catalog can contribute valuable insights regarding data quality. For example, metadata can highlight missing values, outliers, or inconsistencies, which could potentially impact analytics outcomes. Furthermore, some advanced data catalogs provide automated data quality scoring based on predefined criteria, further streamlining the process. By providing these insights, data catalogs empower analysts to make informed decisions about data applicability and the need for data cleaning procedures.

Collaboration and knowledge sharing

A data catalog can foster collaboration among data professionals by serving as a shared platform for knowledge exchange. For instance, data professionals can add annotations or comments to datasets in the catalog, providing additional context or explaining specific transformations applied to the data.

This collaborative aspect can significantly enhance data comprehension, reduce redundancy in efforts, and expedite the analytics process. Over time, the catalog becomes a knowledge repository, building a collective organizational intelligence that enhances data analytics outcomes.

Regulatory compliance

Compliance with data regulations is crucial in the current data-centric business environment. Data catalogs can simplify compliance by maintaining detailed records of data lineage, usage, ownership, and consent. These records can be crucial in audits or regulatory inquiries, ensuring that data analytics processes align with data governance standards.

Data catalogs and business intelligence

In the context of BI, a data catalog can be instrumental in creating a data-driven culture. BI involves converting raw data into actionable insights, a process that relies heavily on data accessibility, understanding, and trust – all of which are facilitated by a data catalog.

The data catalog's role becomes even more crucial in self-service BI models, where non-technical users need to access and understand data for their analytics needs. The catalog's searchability and contextual information empower these users to locate and comprehend relevant data, enabling them to derive insights independently.

Furthermore, BI tools can be integrated with data catalogs, enabling direct data import and enhancing the overall efficiency of BI workflows. This integration ensures that users have the most up-to-date, trusted data for their BI applications.

A data catalog is an essential tool for enhancing data analytics. It improves data discoverability, comprehension, quality, collaboration, and regulatory compliance. In the BI context, a data catalog not only optimizes workflows but also drives a data-driven culture by enabling data access and understanding for all users. In the era of Big Data, a data catalog can be the critical enabler that organizations need to harness their data potential fully.

Data catalogs in data-driven decision making

The role of Data Catalogs in data-driven decision-making is vast. A well-managed Data Catalog aids in data discovery, understanding, and governance, leading to efficient and reliable data analytics and, in turn, more intelligent and accurate business decisions. Let's examine these aspects in more detail.

One of the main issues facing businesses today is the data deluge. Organizations produce and store massive amounts of data in varied formats from myriad sources, making it difficult for data consumers (data analysts, scientists, and business users) to discover the exact data they need. A Data Catalog mitigates this challenge by providing a searchable repository where users can quickly locate relevant data sets for their analytics needs.

The Data Catalog indexes all data assets across an organization, providing detailed metadata about each resource – its source, how it's used, who's using it, its format, its quality, etc. Users can quickly search and discover data based on these parameters, significantly cutting down on time spent in locating the correct data, thus improving the efficiency of data-driven decision-making processes.

Locating the correct data set is only part of the challenge; understanding it is another. Often, data from different sources have different semantics, making it difficult to understand and interpret. A Data Catalog addresses this by providing rich contextual information about the data. This could include definitions, descriptions, annotations, and lineage information.

Data Catalogs also encourage collaboration among users. Users can share insights, ask questions, and provide comments and reviews about data sets, further enhancing the collective understanding of data within the organization. This democratization of data understanding paves the way for more accurate and effective data analytics, supporting informed decision-making.

Data Governance ensures that high data standards are met concerning data quality, privacy, security, and compliance. A Data Catalog is a fundamental tool for effective data governance. It gives a unified view of the organization's data, highlighting any data quality issues, identifying redundant data, and ensuring data is used responsibly.

Through a Data Catalog, organizations can track data lineage, which is crucial for regulatory compliance and data quality assurance. Data lineage helps in understanding where the data originates, how it moves and transforms through systems, and how it's used, thereby establishing trust in the data. When data consumers trust their data, their analyses and subsequent decisions based on that data are more confident and assertive. Moreover, a Data Catalog also helps in data privacy and security. With metadata tagging, sensitive data can be flagged, and appropriate access controls can be enforced. This ensures that sensitive information is only accessed by authorized personnel, thereby complying with data privacy regulations.

Enabling data analytics and BI

Data Catalogs play a pivotal role in enhancing data analytics and BI. They provide the infrastructure that enables users to swiftly locate, understand, and trust their data, which are vital prerequisites for any successful data analytics initiative.

Through a Data Catalog, data preparation for analytics becomes faster and more reliable. Users can identify the most suitable and trusted datasets for their analyses, understand their context, and easily combine them to derive insights. With improved data discovery, understanding, and governance, the quality and reliability of these insights significantly increase.

Moreover, BI tools can integrate with Data Catalogs, leveraging their metadata for enhanced reporting and visualization. With more reliable data and contextual information at their disposal, these tools can deliver more accurate, insightful, and actionable business reports and dashboards.

A Data Catalog is a critical tool in the realm of data-driven decision-making. It enhances data discovery, understanding, and governance, ultimately leading to improved data analytics and BI. By fostering a robust data culture, a Data Catalog helps organizations unlock their data's true potential, enabling smarter, data-driven decisions that drive business success.

Key learnings

A data catalog facilitates data discovery, understanding, and governance, leading to efficient and reliable data analytics and, consequently, smarter and more accurate business decisions.

Data catalogs play a crucial role in enhancing data analytics and BI. They make data more accessible to a diverse range of users across an organization, fostering a data-driven culture.

A data catalog enriches metadata with a business context, providing more depth to the data. Understanding the context of data is crucial for accurate and reliable analytics.

In the context of BI, a data catalog optimizes workflows and drives a data-driven culture by enabling data access and understanding for all users.

A well-managed data catalog can assist in managing data privacy, ensuring compliance with data regulations, and maintaining data quality by documenting the lineage and lifecycle of data assets.

PART VI

Future Trends in Data Cataloging

CHAPTER 15

Artificial Intelligence in Data Cataloging

The term "Artificial Intelligence" has dominated various fields over the past couple of years, contributing to considerable technological progression and improved operational productivity. Nonetheless, it is vital to recognize and comprehend its different variants as we delve more profoundly into the AI realm.

Traditional AI versus generative AI

An emerging form known as Generative AI, a type of AI, holds remarkable potential to transform industries. But how does it distinguish itself from conventional AI?

Traditional AI

Traditional AI, also referred to as Narrow or Weak Artificial Intelligence, concentrates on executing a specific task intelligently. These are systems constructed to respond to a distinct range of inputs. They possess the ability to learn from data, making decisions or predictions rooted in this data. Consider playing a chess game on a computer. The computer understands all the rules, anticipates your moves, and plans its own moves based on an established strategy. It doesn't innovate new ways to play chess, but selects from strategies it has been programmed with. That's the essence of Traditional AI—it's akin to a proficient strategist making informed decisions within a given set of guidelines. Voice assistants like Siri or Alexa, Netflix or Amazon's recommendation engines, or Google's search algorithm are all instances of Traditional AI. They are conditioned to adhere to specific rules, perform a precise task, and do it effectively, though they can't produce anything novel.

Generative AI

Contrastingly, Generative AI is the latest phase of artificial intelligence. It's a version of AI that can generate something fresh. Imagine having a friend who excels at narrating stories. However, instead of a human companion, you have an AI. You offer this AI a beginning line like, "Once upon a time, in a galaxy far away…". AI develops this line into an entire space odyssey story, brimming with characters, unexpected turns, and a thrilling finale. AI crafts something new from the information you provide. This is a fundamental representation of Generative AI—it resembles a creative friend who can devise original content. Moreover, present-day Generative AI is not limited to text outputs but can also generate images, music, and even computer code. They are trained on a data set, comprehending underlying patterns to produce new data reflective of the training set.

Take GPT-4, OpenAI's language prediction model, as a stellar example of Generative AI. Trained on extensive portions of the internet, it can create human-like text nearly indistinguishable from a person's writing.

The fundamental distinction

The critical disparity between traditional and Generative AI resides in their capacities and applications. Traditional AI systems are chiefly employed to scrutinize data and forecast outcomes, whereas Generative AI takes a step further by generating new data resembling its training data.

In simpler terms, Traditional AI is proficient in pattern recognition, while Generative AI excels in pattern creation. Traditional AI can analyze data and interpret what it encounters, while Generative AI can utilize the same data to generate something completely new.

Generative AI has far-reaching implications, opening up new paths for creativity and innovation. In the design sector, it can aid in creating numerous prototypes in a few minutes, decreasing the time consumed in the ideation process. In the entertainment field, it can assist in producing new music, writing scripts, or even crafting deepfakes. In journalism, it could pen articles or reports. Generative AI holds the potential to revolutionize any sector where creation and innovation are paramount.

Meanwhile, Traditional AI continues to dominate task-specific applications. It drives our chatbots, recommendation systems, predictive analytics, and much more. It is the driving force behind the majority of current AI applications, optimizing efficiencies across various sectors.

Although Traditional AI and Generative AI have distinct functions, they are not incompatible. Generative AI could collaborate with Traditional AI to deliver even more robust solutions. For instance, Traditional AI could analyze user behavior data, and Generative AI could utilize this analysis to produce personalized content.

As we continue to discover the immense potential of AI, comprehending these differences is crucial. Both Generative and Traditional AI have significant roles in molding our future, each offering unique possibilities. Adopting these cutting-edge technologies is crucial for businesses and individuals striving to maintain a competitive edge in our swiftly advancing digital environment.

AI-driven data cataloging techniques

The evolution of AI has precipitated significant advancements in data management strategies, including data cataloging. These methods, driven by sophisticated AI algorithms, can transform how businesses catalog, manage, and utilize their data, paving the way for more intelligent decision-making processes.

AI-powered data catalogs

Traditional data catalogs are structured systems that provide an organized inventory of data assets, incorporating information about data sources, lineage, usage, and more. However, their reliance on manual processes for data classification, tagging, and metadata management can be burdensome and prone to errors.

On the other hand, AI-driven data catalogs harness the power of ML and NLP to automate and refine these processes. AI-enhanced catalogs can identify, classify, and tag data automatically, reducing the risk of human error and significantly streamlining catalog management. Further, they can understand and learn from user interactions, continuously improving their performance over time.

Automatic data classification and tagging

AI-driven data cataloging begins with the automatic classification and tagging of data. Machine learning algorithms are used to scan and analyze datasets, identify critical attributes and patterns, and then classify and tag the data accordingly. This process, which would be time-consuming and labor-intensive if performed manually, is accelerated and made more accurate with AI.

For instance, we can use unsupervised learning techniques like clustering to group similar data. In contrast, we can use supervised learning techniques to identify and tag specific features based on pre-existing labels. Additionally, we can use NLP to interpret and tag unstructured data, such as text, and even to derive meaningful insights from it.

Deep Learning (DL) can significantly enhance data classification and tagging processes. Deep learning algorithms, such as Convolutional Neural Networks (CNN) and Recurrent Neural Networks (RNN), can extract complex patterns and relationships from high-dimensional datasets.

For example, consider a dataset with millions of records spanning a multitude of fields, such as a customer transaction database. A Convolutional Neural Network (CNN) could analyze this data, identifying complex patterns that correspond to various customer behaviors, and tag the data accordingly. Meanwhile, Recurrent Neural

Networks (RNN), with its ability to handle sequential data, could analyze time-series data like stock prices or weather data, classifying and tagging them based on temporal patterns.

Metadata management and data lineage with graph theory

AI can also greatly enhance metadata management and data lineage tracking. Metadata is critical for understanding the context, quality, and potential use of a given dataset. Traditional metadata management requires a significant manual effort, but AI-driven methods can automatically generate and update metadata as data evolves.

Similarly, data lineage – the history of data from its origin to its current state – is vital for ensuring data reliability and compliance. AI techniques can automatically track and record data lineage, providing a clear, easily accessible audit trail.

AI-driven metadata management can be further enhanced using graph theory. In this context, data entities (tables, columns, etc.) appear as nodes, and the relationships between them (foreign keys, joins, etc.) appear as edges.

Graph-based models allow for efficient storage, processing, and querying of metadata. For instance, a user could quickly trace back the lineage of a dataset or identify all datasets related to a particular entity with a single graph query.

Furthermore, ML algorithms can be applied to these graph representations for better metadata management. Techniques like node classification or link prediction could help deduce missing metadata or predict new relationships between data entities.

Contextualized and personalized recommendations

AI-driven data catalogs can offer contextualized and personalized data recommendations to users. This is achieved by analyzing users' past data interactions, inferring their needs, and then recommending relevant data assets.

For example, if a user often works with a specific type of data, the AI system could automatically suggest similar or related datasets when the user is searching for data. This could significantly reduce the time and effort required for data discovery and preparation.

Semantic search and data discovery

AI can also be employed to improve data discovery through semantic search. Unlike traditional keyword-based search methods, semantic search understands the context and intent behind search queries, delivering more accurate and relevant results.

With semantic search, users can find data based on its meaning and context rather than just its label. For example, a user could search for "customer transaction data for last quarter," and the AI system could understand this complex query, locating the relevant datasets even if they aren't explicitly labeled with these exact words.

Semantic search can be made even more effective with Transformer-based models. These models, including BERT (Bidirectional Encoder Representations from Transformers), have been proven effective in capturing the contextual meaning of words and sentences.

When applied to data cataloging, these models can be trained to understand the semantics of complex search queries, allowing users to search for data in a more intuitive, conversational manner. This represents a significant improvement over traditional keyword-based search methods, which lack this level of sophistication and flexibility.

Anomaly detection and data quality management

AI-driven data cataloging can also assist in data quality management by detecting anomalies and inconsistencies in data. By continuously monitoring datasets, AI systems can identify outliers, missing values, incorrect data entries, and other issues that could compromise data quality.

Once an anomaly is detected, the system can either automatically correct it (if possible) or alert users to the issue, allowing them to address it promptly. This not only ensures the accuracy and reliability of the data but also prevents potential problems from propagating through downstream analytics processes.

These techniques range from statistical methods, like the Z-score or IQR methods, to more complex ML models, like Autoencoders or Isolation Forests.

For instance, Autoencoders, a type of neural network, could be used to model the "normal" state of a dataset. When new data comes in, the model attempts to reconstruct it based on what it has learned. If the reconstruction error is beyond a certain threshold, the new data is marked as an anomaly.

The advent of AI and ML technologies is reshaping the landscape of data cataloging, making it more efficient, accurate, and user-friendly. These advancements are not only streamlining existing processes but also enabling new capabilities that were previously unachievable. As AI technologies continue to evolve, they will undoubtedly unlock even more potential in the field of data cataloging.

AI-powered data discovery and recommendations

As the magnitude and complexity of data continue to grow, the way organizations manage, understand, and leverage this asset also needs to evolve. Data cataloging has historically been a time-consuming and manual task, often unable to keep pace with the escalating influx of data. However, AI-powered data discovery and recommendations are redefining the data cataloging landscape, ushering in a new era of augmented data management.

AI-powered data discovery is about the automated or semi-automated exploration of data or content to find patterns, trends, and correlations that are otherwise invisible to the naked eye. ML algorithms underpin this technology, scanning structured, semi-structured, and unstructured data to extract valuable insights. The applications of AI-powered data discovery span a wide range of techniques:

- **Cluster analysis.** This unsupervised ML technique groups sets of objects in such a way that objects in the same group (a cluster) are more similar to each other than to those in other groups (clusters). Cluster analysis is instrumental in market segmentation, social network analysis, and image segmentation.

- **Regression analysis.** Regression techniques predict the relationship between dependent and independent variables. In the context of AI-powered data discovery, regression can be used to predict outcomes based on historical data.

- **Classification analysis**. This method categorizes data into various classes or categories. Classification models using algorithms like decision trees, logistic regression, or neural networks can predict discrete responses—for example, whether an email is spam or not.

- **Time series analysis**. AI-powered data discovery can also help understand time-series data and forecast future values based on historical data.

AI-powered data recommendations leverage ML to suggest contextually relevant and valuable insights. This technology is about recommending the most fitting datasets for specific queries based on user behavior and interaction history with the data. AI data recommendations can take several forms:

- **Dataset recommendations**. AI can analyze a user's historical data interaction and suggest relevant datasets for a new query or task. It helps save time and ensures the use of the most fitting data, thereby improving the quality of insights.

- **Analytical recommendations**. Based on the selected dataset, AI can suggest the type of analysis that would be most appropriate, aiding users in making the most of their data.

- **Predictive recommendations.** Using the power of AI, organizations can make predictions about future trends and outcomes based on current and historical data.

Integrating AI-powered data discovery and recommendations brings a transformative approach to data cataloging:

- **Automated data cataloging.** Using ML algorithms, AI can automate the process of data cataloging. It can learn from existing data classifications and apply those rules to new, uncategorized data. This not only saves time but also creates a more consistent and accurate data catalog.

- **Data quality enhancement.** AI can identify anomalies, inconsistencies, and gaps in data. With time, it can even learn to rectify them, leading to an overall improvement in data quality. This minimizes the effort required for data cleaning and pre-processing, freeing data scientists to focus on more valuable tasks.

- **Improved data accessibility.** NLP, a branch of AI, can make data more accessible to non-technical users. With NLP, users can interact with data using everyday language, and AI can comprehend the context, semantics, and intent of the query to return accurate results.

- **Smart recommendations**. AI can provide smart recommendations on the most suitable datasets for specific queries. By understanding user intent and analyzing the query, AI can suggest relevant datasets, reducing data exploration time.

- **Predictive analysis**. AI also offers predictive capabilities, enabling organizations to anticipate future trends and make proactive decisions.

NLP in data cataloging

As we look toward the future, the potential of AI in data cataloging is boundless:

- **Advanced machine learning techniques**. Techniques such as deep learning and reinforcement learning will enable more sophisticated pattern recognition and predictive modeling. This will enhance the accuracy and value of insights derived from data.

- **Improved predictive capabilities**. As AI models become more sophisticated, their predictive capabilities will also enhance. This will allow organizations to anticipate future trends with greater precision and confidence.

- **Enhanced data privacy and governance.** AI will play a crucial role in data privacy and governance. Techniques like differential privacy will allow organizations to utilize and share data without compromising privacy. AI will also streamline data governance by tracking data lineage and usage and maintaining data integrity, thus ensuring regulatory compliance.

AI-powered data discovery and recommendations are poised to revolutionize data cataloging. By transforming traditional processes and accelerating decision-making, AI is set to drive the future of data management. Through automation, increased data quality, and predictive capabilities, organizations will harness their data assets like never before, enabling unprecedented levels of insight, efficiency, and agility.

The ubiquity of unstructured data generated globally, especially in text form, has increased the need to harvest and process this data. This data includes user-generated content, reviews, comments, notes, and a wealth of information from different sources. While this data offers an unprecedented opportunity for extracting value, its high-volume, high-velocity, and high-variety nature makes processing it a challenging task.

NLP is a critical AI subset that empowers machines to understand, interpret, and make sense of human languages, bringing transformative changes to data cataloging practices. The following is an in-depth exploration of how NLP plays a crucial role in the future of data cataloging.

The advent of NLP has been pivotal in shaping the future of data cataloging, primarily through its roles in:

- **Data discovery**. Data discovery is the process of finding and understanding data relevant to a particular requirement. NLP algorithms, like word embeddings (Word2Vec, GloVe), can capture semantic relationships between words and can be used to analyze and interpret metadata, facilitating automated and intelligent data discovery. Advanced techniques such as contextualized word embeddings (like BERT, GPT, ELMo) allow for even better handling of language nuances and understanding of the context and semantics of the data.

- **Data classification**. For data classification, NLP offers a range of algorithms and techniques. Topic modeling algorithms like Latent Dirichlet Allocation (LDA) can classify documents into different topics based on word frequency. Named Entity Recognition (NER) is another powerful tool that can classify named entities in text into predefined categories like persons, organizations, locations, etc. This automated categorization of data aids in generating structured insights from unstructured data.

- **Data quality control.** Ensuring data quality is crucial to the validity of insights derived from it. NLP can help identify errors or inconsistencies in text data that may impact the quality of analysis. Techniques like text normalization, spell-checking, and grammar-checking can spot and correct anomalies in the data. Furthermore, sentiment analysis can be used to detect any potential biases in the data, and techniques like outlier detection can help identify irrelevant content.

- **Semantic search.** NLP significantly enhances the search function of data catalogs. Traditional keyword-based search methods are often insufficient as they lack an understanding of the contextual meaning. However, by implementing NLP, a semantic search can be achieved. Techniques such as semantic similarity and intent recognition enable search tools to interpret the user's query in a more context-aware and human-like manner, providing more accurate and relevant results.

NLP, in conjunction with AI and advanced analytics, can transform the way we catalog and interact with data:

- **Automated metadata generation.** Through NLP, AI can automatically generate metadata for unstructured data. It can extract critical topics, named entities, and sentiments, reducing the effort for metadata generation. Techniques such as extractive or abstractive summarization can be used to provide a brief overview of the documents, further aiding in understanding the context of the data.

- **Contextual understanding and semantic analysis.** By employing NLP, AI systems can understand the context of data far beyond pattern recognition or simple keyword matching. Techniques such as sentiment analysis, emotion detection, sarcasm detection, etc., can help understand the underlying tone and sentiment of the data. Transformers models like BERT, GPT-3, etc., provide a deep contextual understanding by capturing the dependencies between words in a sentence, leading to deeper and more meaningful analysis.

- **Data lineage and provenance.** Understanding the origin, relationships, and transformations of data over time is essential for maintaining data integrity and trustworthiness. NLP can parse and interpret notes and comments associated with datasets, revealing their lineage and provenance.

- **Anomaly detection.** Advanced analytics can use NLP to detect anomalies in text data, such as sudden shifts in sentiment or topic. Time-series analysis of text data using NLP can reveal trends and anomalies that might indicate emerging trends or data quality issues.

- **Improving accessibility**. By utilizing NLP, data catalogs can become more accessible and user-friendly. Natural language queries, instead of complex query languages, can be used to find and interact with data. Techniques like text simplification can make complex data sets more understandable for non-experts.

NLP is a transformative technology reshaping the future of data cataloging. Its ability to read, understand, and generate human languages opens up limitless possibilities for processing unstructured data and turning it into actionable insights. As we move forward, the convergence of NLP, AI, and advanced analytics will create more intelligent, efficient, and user-friendly data catalogs capable of providing valuable insights at scale. The growth and evolution of NLP technologies are set to revolutionize data cataloging even further, necessitating an in-depth understanding and adoption of these powerful tools in data management strategies.

The role of generative AI in data cataloging

Generative AI, encompassing technologies such as Generative Adversarial Networks (GANs) and transformer models, is rapidly redefining the landscape of data cataloging. This exciting convergence represents a significant shift, intertwining two fields known for their complexity and transformative potential. It's a frontier rich with opportunities for growth, innovation, and impact, yet fraught with multifaceted challenges that demand a thoughtful approach.

The relationship between these two domains is not just a technological feat but a complex interplay involving technology, ethics, society, and the environment. It's a field bursting with potential, yet one that requires responsible stewardship:

- **Technological considerations**. Generative AI is forging new paths in data cataloging, from the use of Generative Adversarial Networks (GANs) for data augmentation to transformer models that enable Natural Language Queries (NLQ). The horizon is dotted with cutting-edge techniques that continue to redefine the field.

- **Ethical considerations.** The integration of Generative AI brings to the fore critical ethical issues, including bias, privacy, and security. These must be navigated with both care and foresight to ensure responsible development.

- **Societal considerations.** This technology can potentially foster more transparent, accessible, and equitable data ecosystems. Careful deployment can align these innovations with societal values and regulations, making them more beneficial to all.

- **Environmental considerations.** It's vital to recognize the environmental footprint of AI models. Thoughtful strategies for reducing energy consumption and embracing sustainable practices are an essential part of the development landscape.

However, this promising path is not without its obstacles. The challenges are complex and require a nuanced, multidisciplinary approach. Success hinges on a collective dedication to excellence, responsibility, inclusivity, and continuous learning.

By embracing these principles and actively engaging with the intricate web of complexities and opportunities, the community of researchers, practitioners, policymakers, and stakeholders can ensure that Generative AI in data cataloging becomes a catalyst for positive transformation. This effort has the potential to resonate not only within the field of Data Catalogs but also across the broader spectrum of human progress and endeavor.

Key learnings

AI significantly enhances data cataloging, introducing more intelligent, automated, and streamlined processes that impact Business Intelligence (BI) by driving shifts toward smarter data management and usage.

Data discovery in data catalogs, which involves efficient navigation and data retrieval methods within extensive catalogs, is pivotal for saving time, enhancing data accessibility, and enabling better insights.

Natural Language Processing (NLP) improves data discoverability and user interaction in data catalogs by making them more intuitive and allowing users to search using Natural Language Queries (NLQ).

AI-powered suggestions in data catalogs could suggest relevant data or insights to users based on their usage patterns or queries, enhancing user experience and operational efficiency.

CHAPTER 16

Blockchain and Data Cataloging

With data becoming an invaluable asset, its provenance and trustworthiness have assumed paramount importance. The data lineage and history are fundamental for the effective application of data in various fields, such as analytics, ML, and decision-making. A robust solution to ensure data provenance and trustworthiness is by leveraging blockchain technology.

Blockchain, a decentralized and distributed ledger technology, brings an added layer of security and transparency by ensuring the immutability and traceability of transactions. In the context of data cataloging, blockchain can significantly enhance the reliability and integrity of data, therefore, improving trust among stakeholders.

Data provenance and the role of blockchain

Data provenance involves tracing the origin, ownership, and transformation history of data, serving as the data's "metadata fingerprint." By ensuring data provenance, we can answer crucial questions about the data, such as:

Where *did the data originate?*

Who has owned or controlled the data throughout its life cycle?

What transformations have the data undergone?

Blockchain technology enhances data provenance through its inherent characteristics:

- **Decentralization**. Unlike traditional centralized systems, where a single authority controls and validates transactions, blockchain operates on a peer-to-peer network where multiple nodes participate in the process. Each node maintains an independent copy of the entire ledger, contributing to the decentralization and distributed nature of the system. This structure makes the system highly resilient against single points of failure or data tampering, reinforcing the reliability of the data provenance.

- **Transparency**. Every transaction in a blockchain network is transparent and visible to all participating nodes. This transparency ensures that the history of data – from its origin to its current state – is open for all participants to see and verify, thus enhancing the data's provenance.

- **Immutability**. Once a transaction is verified and added to a block, modifying or deleting that information is practically impossible. Each block in the blockchain is linked to the previous one via a unique identifier (hash), which changes if any transaction within the block changes. This mechanism ensures that any attempt to modify a transaction will break the entire chain, ensuring the immutability of the blockchain and, by extension, the permanence of the data provenance.

Trust in blockchain

The role of blockchain in building trust is fundamentally linked to its unique characteristics: consensus mechanisms, transparency, and cryptographic security.

Consensus mechanisms such as Proof-of-Work or Proof-of-Stake ensure that all transactions are agreed upon by the majority of nodes in the network before being recorded on the blockchain. This democratic process prevents any single entity from manipulating the transaction record, creating a system where trust is embedded within the protocol itself rather than relying on intermediaries or third parties.

The transparency of blockchain, coupled with cryptographic security, ensures that every transaction is transparently recorded and secured against modifications.

The data cannot be tampered with or falsified without detection, thereby increasing trust in the data's authenticity and accuracy among all participants in the network.

Blockchain in the context of data cataloging

Data cataloging refers to managing and organizing data to make it easily discoverable, accessible, and usable. This process involves recording metadata about data assets, such as their location, format, relationships, and usage history. Blockchain's role in data cataloging can revolutionize the way we manage and trust our data assets by improving their:

- **Discoverability**. Blockchain can enhance data discoverability by maintaining a decentralized, transparent, and immutable ledger of data assets. Each entry in the ledger (i.e., each data asset) is accompanied by metadata, which is recorded as transactions on the blockchain. This process not only maintains an accurate record of the data asset's lifecycle but also makes this information easily discoverable for users across the network.

- **Verifiability**. Given its inherent immutability and transparency, blockchain provides an efficient mechanism for verifying the authenticity of data assets. Users can trace the entire history of data assets – from their creation to their current state – thereby verifying their origin, transformations, and ownership. This verifiability enhances trust in the data and its metadata, which is critical for data-intensive applications like data analytics and ML.

- **Security and access control**. Blockchain, coupled with smart contracts, can significantly enhance the security and access control of data assets. Smart contracts are self-executing contracts with the terms of the agreement written into code. In the context of data cataloging, they can automate and enforce access permissions to data assets based on predefined rules. This feature ensures that only authorized users can access specific data assets, reducing the risk of data breaches and unauthorized access.

Moreover, the cryptographic security of blockchain technology further safeguards data assets against tampering or theft. Each transaction is encrypted and linked to the previous one through a unique hash, making altering or falsifying data entries extremely challenging.

By leveraging blockchain, we can enable the interoperability of different data catalogs. Interoperability refers to the ability of different systems to work together and exchange information. By recording metadata and data transactions on a standard blockchain, different data catalogs can exchange and verify information more easily. This feature promotes data sharing and collaboration across different platforms and stakeholders while maintaining the trustworthiness and provenance of the data.

As we look toward the future of data cataloging, blockchain emerges as a critical player in ensuring data provenance, fostering trust, and enhancing data management. By leveraging blockchain's unique properties, we can significantly improve data transparency, security, and interoperability, transforming the way we manage and trust our data in the digital age. However, while blockchain holds immense promise, it is crucial to address its challenges – such as scalability, energy consumption, and regulatory issues – to realize its potential in data cataloging and beyond fully.

Implementing blockchain in data catalogs

The concept of implementing blockchain technology in data catalogs presents several transformative opportunities for organizations seeking to maintain data integrity, transparency, and security. However, to fully understand the benefits, it is necessary to grasp how this implementation would function at a technical level. In essence, the blockchain is a distributed ledger that securely records transactions between multiple parties. It is immutable and provides an incorruptible data trail. This inherent security and transparency make it a compelling prospect for enhancing data cataloging operations.

Structuring blocks for data catalogs

A blockchain is a chronological list of records grouped into blocks chained together using cryptography. This structure provides an immutable record of all transactions or changes within a system.

In the context of data catalogs, every data entry or metadata change can be considered a "transaction." The structure of a block should be designed to accommodate these transactions. This could include details such as data schema, a unique identifier for each dataset, data lineage, usage metric, or owner.

Each block includes three key elements: a cryptographic hash of the previous block, a timestamp, and the data transaction. The hash function gives the block a unique identifier, which changes with any alteration in block data.

The data's cryptographic hash and the subsequent linking between blocks make the blockchain inherently secure against tampering, as a change in one block would necessitate changing every block that follows to maintain integrity, making data tampering evident.

When it comes to data cataloging, the blockchain's block structure needs to be customized to accommodate specific data entries and metadata. This might include a unique identifier for each dataset, data schema, data lineage information, data owners, data usage metrics, and more.

Implementing a consensus algorithm

Blockchain systems employ consensus algorithms to agree on the validity of transactions across all network nodes. Standard algorithms include Proof-of-Work (PoW), Proof-of-Stake (PoS), and Delegated Proof-of-Stake (DPoS). Each has its strengths and weaknesses, and the choice largely depends on the particular use-case requirements. For instance, if a system requires low energy consumption and fast transaction time, PoS or DPoS might be more suitable.

In the context of data cataloging, the consensus algorithm would serve to verify changes to the catalog – ensuring that only authorized modifications are made. The particular consensus algorithm chosen would likely depend on the organization's specific needs, such as the need for scalability, speed, or robustness against malicious attacks.

Interacting with the blockchain

To interact with the blockchain for data cataloging purposes, APIs can be built. These APIs would allow users to query the blockchain and retrieve data in a user-friendly manner. These APIs can be designed to support a wide variety of functionalities – for instance, adding new datasets to the catalog, updating metadata, verifying data lineage, and more.

These interfaces can also provide mechanisms for accessing and understanding the provenance and changes in data assets over time. Because all changes are recorded on the immutable blockchain, it offers a clear and secure audit trail.

Ensuring data privacy

Blockchain's inherent transparency can be a double-edged sword. While it promotes accountability and traceability, it could also potentially expose sensitive data. To mitigate this, techniques such as zero-knowledge proofs can be employed. This form of cryptographic proof allows one party to prove to another that they know a value (such as a password or a secret key) without conveying any information apart from the fact that they know the value.

In the context of a data catalog, we can verify that a user has the right to access specific data without revealing the data itself or any additional information.

While implementing blockchain in data catalogs poses specific technical challenges, the potential benefits in terms of enhanced security, accountability, and traceability make it a promising avenue for future exploration. The unique properties of blockchain technology can help facilitate more robust data cataloging practices, thereby enabling more reliable and trustworthy data-driven decision-making.

Challenges and opportunities

As we propel into the future of data cataloging, blockchain technology shows promising prospects in terms of data security, provenance, transparency, and interoperability. However, realizing these opportunities isn't without challenges. This section presents a nuanced perspective on the opportunities and hurdles associated with implementing blockchain in data cataloging.

Challenges include:

- **Scalability and performance**. Although blockchains like Ethereum and Bitcoin are highly secure, they can currently handle only a limited number of transactions per second. Similarly, on-chain data storage in the blockchain is expensive and slower compared to traditional databases. This poses a severe challenge for data cataloging, where large-scale, high-speed data processing is often required.

- **Regulatory and legal concerns.** Data privacy regulations such as GDPR and CCPA present challenges for blockchain implementation. Because blockchain networks are inherently transparent and immutable, they conflict with privacy norms, like the right to be forgotten. Complying with these standards requires innovative solutions that strike a balance between blockchain's transparency and legal requirements.

- **Interoperability.** Many different blockchain protocols exist, each with its own standards. Interoperability — the ability of different blockchain systems to communicate and work together — is a significant technical hurdle. A unified or standard data cataloging practice across these various protocols is not straightforward to implement.

- **Adoption and change management.** Moving from traditional data cataloging methods to blockchain-based systems requires substantial effort and a paradigm shift. It includes dealing with resistance to change, training personnel to operate in a decentralized environment, and updating business processes to align with the new technology.

Opportunities include:

- **Improved data provenance and integrity**. One of the core advantages of blockchain technology is its immutability. Once data is recorded onto a blockchain, it can't be changed, providing a strong guarantee of data integrity. This feature can significantly improve data provenance tracking in data catalogs, providing a clear and unchangeable record of data origin, transformations, and ownership over time.

- **Enhanced security**. Blockchain's decentralized nature and cryptographic algorithms ensure that data cataloging systems are resilient to single-point-of-failure risks and unauthorized data alterations. This can dramatically enhance the security of the data cataloging process, especially in multi-party environments.

- **Increased trust and transparency**. Blockchain provides a shared, unified view of data transactions, ensuring all parties agree on the status of data assets in the catalog. This transparency can increase trust among users and stakeholders, as they can independently verify and audit the data transactions.

- **Facilitate data marketplaces**. Blockchain technology can facilitate the creation of data marketplaces, where data is treated as an asset that can be traded. This introduces a new level of granularity in data access control and monetization, where individual data assets in a catalog can be securely and transparently bought, sold, or licensed.

- **Enable decentralized data catalogs**. Through blockchain, the creation of decentralized data catalogs becomes feasible. In these catalogs, no single party controls the catalog, and updates are performed through a consensus protocol. This decentralization can spur collaboration and shared use of data resources across organizations.

While there are significant challenges to the application of blockchain in data cataloging, the potential benefits make it an area worthy of exploration. The fields of data management and blockchain technology need to evolve together to unlock these opportunities and address the associated challenges fully. Through continued research, innovation, and perhaps some disruption to our traditional way of thinking, the future of data cataloging can be revolutionized through the integration of blockchain technology.

Key learnings

Blockchain can bolster data reliability and integrity in data cataloging, thereby enhancing stakeholder trust, due to its decentralized and distributed ledger technology.

Data provenance, or tracing the origin, ownership, and transformation history of data, acts as its "metadata fingerprint."

The transparency and immutability afforded by blockchain not only enhance data provenance by ensuring a transparent, verifiable history of data but also guarantee the permanence of such provenance by preventing unauthorized data modification.

Blockchain's application in data catalogs can verify user access rights to specific data without revealing the data or additional information, and holds promise for the future of data cataloging, particularly in ensuring data security, provenance, transparency, and interoperability, by providing a unified, agreed-upon view of data transactions.

CHAPTER 17

Data Catalogs of Tomorrow

As we stand on the precipice of the information era, data continues to grow exponentially in volume, variety, velocity, and veracity. According to the latest available forecast from IDC is that the global data sphere will grow at a compound annual growth rate (CAGR) of 21.2% to reach more than 475 zettabytes by 2030.

In this vast sea of data, the capacity for businesses and organizations to effectively manage and extract meaningful insights is more critical than ever. One key aspect of this data management challenge is data cataloging. As we look ahead, several trends and technologies will shape the future of data cataloging, potentially transforming the way businesses catalog, discover, and manage their data assets.

Artificial intelligence and machine learning

Automated metadata management, powered by AI and ML, will form the bedrock of the next generation of data cataloging solutions. These technologies will enable more dynamic, intelligent, and contextually-aware data catalogs, which can understand the relationship and significance of various data elements automatically. Automated data cataloging solutions will employ NLP and semantic discovery to understand and interpret complex data, as well as automatic tagging, categorizing, and enriching metadata, reducing the time and effort required for manual metadata management.

Data privacy and security by design

With stringent data privacy regulations, such as the GDPR and CCPA, and the constant threat of cyberattacks, data cataloging solutions will need to integrate data privacy and security considerations by design. Techniques such as anonymization and pseudonymization will be fundamental in cataloging data without compromising privacy. In the future, we can expect data catalogs to be equipped with intelligent features like access control, auditing, and data lineage to ensure proper governance and compliance.

Integration with data management and analytics platforms

As businesses continue to leverage a variety of data management tools (data lakes, data warehouses, and data hubs) and analytics platforms (BI tools and AI platforms), integration capability will become crucial for data catalogs. Future data cataloging solutions will be built with APIs and connectors to easily integrate with a wide range of third-party platforms and tools, enabling a single source of truth and a seamless data pipeline across the organization.

Decentralized data catalogs

As organizations become more data-driven and democratize access to data, we may see a shift towards decentralized data catalogs. This means enabling every department or even individual users to maintain and manage their own data catalogs that align with their specific needs while also ensuring proper data governance and security. This trend aligns with the broader trend towards decentralization in IT and could be facilitated by blockchain technology.

Contextual and personalized data catalogs

Personalization is critical to enhancing user experience and productivity in many domains, and data cataloging is no exception. Future data catalogs could leverage AI and ML to provide contextual and personalized recommendations, helping users discover relevant datasets and insights based on their roles, interests, and previous activities.

Real-time data cataloging

With the increasing adoption of real-time data processing and analytics, data cataloging will need to keep pace. Real-time data cataloging will enable businesses to immediately catalog and make sense of streaming data, facilitating real-time decision-making and analytics.

The future of data cataloging holds significant promise and is poised to play a critical role in shaping how businesses manage, discover, and extract value from their growing data assets. However, realizing this vision will require a concerted effort from technology providers, businesses, and regulators to address the technical, organizational, and regulatory challenges that lie ahead.

Embracing data-centric culture

As organizations increasingly shift towards data-driven decision-making, adopting a data-centric culture becomes paramount. This implies promoting data transparency, data accessibility, data literacy, and a shared understanding of data as a valuable asset. Within this context, data cataloging plays a vital role in fostering a data-centric culture.

Data cataloging holds immense importance in promoting a data-centric culture for several reasons:

- **Data accessibility and discovery**. A comprehensive data catalog ensures that data is easily accessible and discoverable. Employees, regardless of their technical prowess, can locate relevant data and leverage it for their tasks. This reduces time spent searching for data, increasing efficiency and productivity.

- **Promoting data literacy**. A data catalog helps users understand the data context, its origin, transformations, and uses. It fosters an environment where individuals can comprehend and use data effectively, thereby improving data literacy across the organization.

- **Data governance and quality**. Data catalogs enhance data governance capabilities by providing insight into the data's lineage, usage, and transformations. This aids in maintaining data quality and compliance, essential aspects of a data-centric culture.

- **Facilitating collaboration**. Through a data catalog, users can share, collaborate, and reuse data assets more effectively. It helps foster a communal environment where data is viewed as a shared asset.

To successfully integrate data cataloging into a data-centric culture, organizations can follow these steps:

- **Define clear goals and objectives**. Start by establishing clear objectives for the data catalog. This could range from improving data discovery to enhancing compliance or fostering data literacy. The objectives will guide the data cataloging process and its integration with organizational culture.

- **Choose the right tools**. Several data cataloging tools are available in the market, each with its own strengths and weaknesses. Choose a tool that aligns with the organization's needs, is user-friendly, and can be easily integrated with the existing data infrastructure.

- **Involve stakeholders**. Stakeholders from different departments should be involved in creating and maintaining the data catalog. This not only ensures that the catalog is comprehensive and relevant but also promotes data literacy and ownership among stakeholders.

- **Promote data stewardship**. Appoint data stewards responsible for maintaining the data catalog, ensuring data quality, and promoting its use within the organization. This can be crucial in ensuring the sustained value of the data catalog.

- **Regularly update the data catalog**. A data catalog is not a one-time effort. It must be updated regularly to reflect new data sources, transformations, and uses. Regular updates ensure that the catalog remains relevant and valuable.

- **Measure success**. Lastly, monitor the use and effectiveness of the data catalog using defined metrics. This will help gauge whether the data catalog meets its intended objectives and promotes a data-centric culture.

Embracing a data-centric culture is a journey that requires thoughtful steps. Data cataloging is a powerful tool that can pave the way toward this culture, facilitating data accessibility, promoting data literacy, enhancing data governance, and fostering collaboration. The key is to align the data catalog with the organization's objectives, involve all stakeholders, and ensure its regular maintenance and updating.

Driving innovation through data catalogs

The ascendancy of data as the primary resource powering the digital age necessitates a revolutionary approach toward its storage, processing, and management. Central to this endeavor is the implementation of a data catalog, a crucial tool that creates an organized inventory of data assets through meticulous metadata management. More than just a data management tool, data catalogs serve as a catalyst for innovation, offering an environment that democratizes data access, uncovers unseen insights, enables collaboration, and underpins cutting-edge AI and ML initiatives.

Democratizing data access

Historically, access to data has been reserved for a select few, often housed in departmental silos or concealed within complex systems. This type of environment stifles innovation by creating bottlenecks and inhibiting broad-based insight generation. A data catalog flips this model on its head by democratizing data access, making it easily discoverable, understandable, and usable for all organizational stakeholders.

Detailed metadata, business glossaries, and user-friendly interfaces allow every user to engage with the organization's data, enhancing overall data literacy. This shift in accessibility empowers employees at all levels to generate insights that drive innovation. By creating a unified and democratized data environment, data catalogs foster a culture of curiosity and exploration, inviting innovative problem-solving and informed decision-making.

Uncovering hidden insights

Data catalogs go beyond being mere data inventories. They offer a granular understanding of the data's origin, its transformations, and its potential uses. This is achieved through features like data lineage, data profiling, and business glossary.

Data lineage can reveal the journey of data through systems and processes, illuminating its lifecycle and context. It enables users to trace errors back to their source, improving data quality and consistency. This lineage can highlight patterns and inefficiencies in data transformation processes that could be potential areas for innovation.

Data profiling, the examination of individual data elements and their associated structures, helps understand the quality of the data. It can reveal patterns, correlations, and anomalies within data sets that may lead to new insights, pointing the way to innovative solutions.

A business glossary is a valuable tool for organizations, offering a centralized repository of standardized definitions for key business terms and terminology. Its benefits are multifaceted, ranging from improved communication and collaboration across departments to enhanced data governance and regulatory compliance. By providing a shared understanding of terminology, a business glossary helps prevent misunderstandings, reduces errors, and streamlines decision-making processes. It also facilitates data integration and reporting, making it easier for businesses to harness the full potential of their data assets. Moreover, in an era of increasing data privacy regulations, a well-maintained business glossary can aid in ensuring compliance and mitigating risks associated with data management, ultimately promoting efficiency, transparency, and alignment within the organization.

Facilitating collaboration

In an increasingly interconnected world, the ability to collaborate effectively is a crucial driver of innovation. Data catalogs can act as a shared platform where teams can collaborate and share their understanding of data. By creating a unified view of the organization's data, data catalogs break down silos, leading to cross-pollination of ideas between departments.

Collaborative features such as user ratings, annotations, and discussion threads allow for the sharing of experiences and insights about different data sets. This crowdsourced wisdom is invaluable in finding innovative uses for data, preventing redundancy, and optimizing the overall value derived from the data. For instance, insights derived from a dataset by a marketing analyst can inform product development, leading to data-driven and innovative product design.

Supporting AI and ML initiatives

Data catalogs are critical to the success of AI and ML initiatives, which require high-quality, well-defined data. By maintaining a well-organized catalog of curated data assets, data catalogs ensure that AI and ML models are trained with high-fidelity data, maximizing their performance.

Advanced data catalogs integrate AI capabilities to automate data cataloging tasks like data classification, tagging, and anomaly detection. These AI-driven tasks improve the efficiency and accuracy of the cataloging process while freeing up data professionals for higher-order tasks. It sets up a virtuous cycle where AI improves the data catalog, and the enriched data catalog, in turn, drives more sophisticated AI initiatives.

As organizations navigate the data-intensive landscape of the digital age, a data catalog can be a beacon, guiding them toward informed decision-making and innovative practices. Data catalogs not only create a streamlined, holistic view of an organization's data assets but also foster a culture of data democratization, collaboration, and curiosity.

However, deriving value from a data catalog goes beyond mere implementation. A robust data governance framework is critical to ensure data quality, privacy, and compliance. Furthermore, upskilling employees and cultivating a data-driven mindset across all organizational levels will maximize the potential benefits of a data catalog.

In driving innovation, data catalogs' power lies not only in their ability to unearth new insights but also in reshaping organizations' approach to data. By establishing transparency, fostering collaboration, and nurturing a culture of data-driven decision-making, data catalogs can indeed steer organizations toward an innovative and data-centric future.

The continuing evolution of data cataloging

The role and scope of data cataloging have drastically evolved over the past decade. The proliferation of data from diverse sources, the rising need for data privacy and security, and the advent of innovative technologies have dramatically reshaped the data cataloging landscape.

Automated data cataloging

Automated data cataloging has ushered in a paradigm shift in data management. ML and AI algorithms are increasingly leveraged to classify data types, recognize patterns, identify data anomalies, and suggest metadata tags.

Automation enhances cataloging speed, reduces human error, and facilitates real-time cataloging. However, the effectiveness of automation heavily relies on the quality and relevance of the training data, necessitating regular audits and fine-tuning to ensure accuracy. Future advancements might incorporate adaptive ML algorithms that learn and improve from each cataloging iteration, enhancing their precision over time.

Enhanced metadata management

Metadata management has seen a radical transformation with the use of ontology and semantic technology to capture diverse metadata types. Modern metadata models encapsulate a wide array of metadata, including descriptive, administrative, and technical metadata. They provide a detailed context of the data, aiding its discovery, management, and utilization.

Emerging metadata management platforms offer automatic metadata extraction, metadata versioning, and bulk metadata editing, marking a significant leap in metadata management. Future platforms could further enhance metadata's dynamism and extensibility, enabling real-time metadata updates and augmenting metadata's role in driving data interpretability.

Integration of data catalogs with other data tools

Data catalogs now operate in symbiosis with other data management and analytics tools. They interact seamlessly with data warehouses, data lakes, BI tools, and ETL tools, integrating cataloged data across various data lifecycle stages.

The use of APIs for programmatic access to catalog data enables data scientists and developers to query and retrieve data from the catalog within their code, thereby streamlining data access and promoting data reuse. Future developments could see the integration of catalogs with more tools, fostering a unified, end-to-end data management ecosystem.

Advanced data lineage and provenance

Modern data catalogs offer sophisticated data lineage capabilities to track the data journey across systems and transformations. This includes capturing transformation logic, intermediate data states, and visualizing the data's genealogy.

Data lineage is critical in maintaining data quality, verifying provenance, and ensuring regulatory compliance. Future catalogs could incorporate automated data lineage correction mechanisms to handle data drifts and maintain an accurate data lineage even in dynamic data environments.

Augmented data cataloging

Augmented data cataloging uses AI and ML for semantic search in catalogs, recommendation engines for suggesting relevant datasets, and anomaly detection algorithms for identifying potential data quality issues. It enhances cataloging speed, accuracy, and efficiency and simplifies data discovery and use.

Future advancements could witness the integration of more AI and ML techniques, like deep learning, to capture complex patterns in data and reinforcement learning to enhance recommendation accuracy in dynamic data environments.

Data cataloging and blockchain

Blockchain technology, with its innate characteristics of immutability, transparency, and decentralization, has promising potential in data cataloging. Blockchain could be used to create a decentralized data catalog, where metadata and data lineage information are stored as transactions on the blockchain.

This setup would ensure data integrity and provenance as once the information is recorded on the blockchain, and it cannot be altered, providing a tamper-proof audit trail. Additionally, the transparency of blockchain transactions can help organizations adhere to data governance policies and regulatory compliance.

Looking ahead, the combination of blockchain and AI could further advance data cataloging. For instance, smart contracts could be used to automate metadata management, and AI algorithms could analyze blockchain transactions to extract insights from cataloged data.

Future of data cataloging

The future of data cataloging will be profoundly influenced by the advent of emerging technologies and the evolving data landscape. Blockchain, quantum computing, and more advanced AI and ML techniques are likely to play crucial roles in shaping next-generation data catalogs.

The integration of blockchain could lead to more secure, transparent, and decentralized data catalogs. Quantum computing might speed up cataloging processes, handle complex data structures, and improve data encryption. Advanced AI and ML techniques could further automate cataloging processes, improve data quality detection, and enhance data discovery and utilization.

However, this evolution won't be without challenges. Issues of data privacy, security, interoperability, and scalability will continue to loom large. Hence, the future of data cataloging will also rely on how effectively these challenges are addressed, paving the way for robust, efficient, and intelligent data cataloging solutions.

Key learnings

The anticipated exponential growth in data volume necessitates efficient management, with AI and ML-powered data cataloging becoming crucial in handling the surge.

An increasing integration of data catalogs with other data management tools and analytics platforms is expected, facilitating a unified data pipeline across entities.

A shift towards decentralized data catalogs may occur, allowing users or departments to manage their own catalogs while adhering to data governance and security protocols.

Personalized and real-time data cataloging, enhancing user experience and supporting real-time analytics and decision-making, could become prevalent.

Data cataloging is pivotal in promoting a data-centric culture, enhancing accessibility, literacy, governance, and collaboration.

Future data cataloging may embrace emerging technologies like blockchain and quantum computing, targeting challenges related to data privacy, security, interoperability, and scalability.

PART VII

Case Studies in Data Cataloging Implementation

CHAPTER 18

Case Studies

This chapter will delve into real-world examples of successful data catalog implementations across various industries. By exploring how diverse organizations adopted, adapted, and benefited from data catalogs, we hope to provide a practical roadmap for data professionals looking to implement data cataloging initiatives in their respective fields.

Global retailer

Managing product information becomes a central concern in the hyper-competitive world of global retail, where the variety and volume of products are expanding exponentially. A retailer's success depends heavily on how quickly and accurately they can process vast amounts of product data from various sources. The complexity is compounded by the need to maintain consistency across multiple channels, including in-store, online platforms, and mobile applications. The case of a leading global retailer struggling with managing its extensive product information shines a spotlight on these challenges and how they can be addressed.

The challenge

A top global retailer with a presence in numerous countries and an expansive online footprint was grappling with an unmanageable plethora of product information. With a catalog encompassing millions of SKUs originating from thousands of different vendors, the complexities in managing product data had reached a critical point.

The problem was not merely the volume of the data but the significant inconsistencies, errors, and duplications that had crept into their various digital properties. This data disarray affected several areas:

- **Operational inefficiency**. The time and resources required to rectify the inconsistencies were enormous, leading to delays and inefficiencies in product listing and marketing.

- **Customer experience**. Inaccurate product information led to confusion and mistrust among customers, impacting their buying decisions and overall satisfaction with the retailer.

- **Compliance risks**. The inconsistencies in product data increased the chances of running afoul of various regulatory requirements related to product descriptions, pricing, and other attributes, leading to potential legal issues.

The solution

Understanding the gravity of the situation, the organization embarked on implementing a robust data cataloging solution. The solution was designed with the following key features:

- **Indexing and cataloging.** A centralized system was created to gather all product data, providing a unified view across different channels and platforms.

- **Metadata management.** The solution employed a systematic approach to metadata management. Data assets were clearly defined, annotated, and tagged for easy discovery. This ensured that different teams could understand the data's context and use it effectively.

- **Integration with existing systems.** The solution was integrated with existing inventory, supply chain, and e-commerce platforms to ensure a seamless flow of accurate data.

- **Automated data cleansing**. Automated tools were employed to identify and rectify inconsistencies, errors, and duplications, thus maintaining the quality of the data.

The outcome

The implementation of the data cataloging solution brought about transformative changes:

- **Reduction in data inconsistency**. By centralizing and maintaining product data, inconsistencies and inaccuracies were drastically reduced.

- **Enhanced operational efficiency**. With a single source of truth for all product data, teams across the organization could access reliable and accurate data, streamlining operations.

- **Improved customer satisfaction**. Accurate product information enhanced the customer's shopping experience, leading to increased trust and satisfaction.

- **Compliance risk mitigation**. By maintaining accurate and consistent product information, the retailer significantly reduced the risk of running into compliance-related issues.

Conclusion

The case of this global retailer underscores the critical role of structured data management in today's complex retail environment. By recognizing the pain points in managing extensive product information and taking decisive action, the retailer not only solved immediate issues but positioned itself for future growth.

The success of this data cataloging initiative demonstrates that strategic investments in technology can pay significant dividends in improving operations, enhancing customer experience, and mitigating risks. It sets a precedent for other organizations facing similar challenges and proves that with a thoughtful approach, even the most daunting data challenges can be overcome.

Healthcare organization

In the dynamic and complex field of healthcare, managing and accessing vast amounts of data is critical. Patient information, treatment records, clinical trial data, and research findings are all vital components that must be managed effectively. However, the healthcare industry often grapples with the challenge of disparate data sources, isolated systems, and a lack of interoperability. This can lead to inefficiencies, hinder collaboration, and, most importantly, affect patient care. The case study of a prominent healthcare institution sheds light on these challenges and demonstrates a path to success through enhanced data accessibility.

The challenge

A leading healthcare institution was facing a challenge shared across the industry – the problem of disparate data sources. Vital information related to patients, including treatment records, clinical trial data, and research studies, were stored in different, isolated systems. The issues this led to were multifaceted:

- **Inefficient data sharing**. The lack of a unified view of data led to delays and complications in sharing information between departments, clinicians, researchers, and other stakeholders.

- **Interoperability issues**. Different systems with varying formats and standards created barriers to seamless integration and collaboration, leading to potential errors and miscommunications.

- **Impact on patient care**. The fragmentation of data meant that healthcare providers did not have a comprehensive view of patient information, affecting the quality and timeliness of care.

The solution

To address these challenges, the institution embarked on implementing a data catalog designed with the following functionalities:

- **Comprehensive indexing**. The catalog served as a comprehensive index for the healthcare institution's data landscape, bringing together disparate sources into a unified view.

- **Data provenance and lineage tracking**. It made it possible to track the origin and flow of data, ensuring the accuracy and reliability of the information.

- **Enhanced collaboration**. The catalog facilitated better collaboration between various stakeholders, enabling data sharing, cross-referencing, and synergistic use of data assets.

- **Integration with existing systems**. The data catalog was integrated with existing medical records, research databases, and other systems to ensure seamless access and use.

The outcome

The successful implementation of the data catalog led to several key improvements:

- **Improved patient outcomes.** Enhanced access to comprehensive and reliable patient data enabled more informed and personalized care, leading to better health outcomes.

- **Fostering innovative medical research.** Researchers were able to uncover meaningful connections between different datasets, fostering innovative research and discovery.

- **Improved clinical decision-making.** Clinicians had ready access to relevant information, leading to more timely and accurate decisions regarding patient care.

Conclusion

The case of this healthcare institution illustrates the transformative power of effective data management in the healthcare industry. By recognizing the challenge of disparate data sources and taking targeted action, the institution was able to enhance patient care and foster innovation.

This initiative stands as a testament to the importance of data accessibility and collaboration in healthcare. It highlights how strategic investments in technology can bridge gaps, facilitate communication, and ultimately lead to better patient care and medical advancements. Other healthcare providers facing similar challenges can draw insights from this case to develop their strategies and build a more integrated and patient-centric data ecosystem.

Financial institution

The financial industry is governed by a complex web of regulations designed to ensure integrity, transparency, and protection of consumer interests. Financial institutions must navigate this intricate regulatory landscape while handling vast amounts of sensitive data, including transactional data, customer information, and market intelligence. Missteps in data management can lead to significant fines, reputational damage, and loss of customer trust. The case study of a leading financial institution illustrates how modern data management techniques can be employed to streamline compliance and safeguard against these risks.

The challenge

A prominent financial institution found itself grappling with the complex task of ensuring regulatory compliance, given the vast amounts of sensitive data it handled. The challenges were manifold:

- **Diverse data landscape**. The institution's data landscape was a mix of various types of data,

314 • Data Cataloging

including transactional data, customer data, and
market data, each with its compliance
requirements.

- **Potential regulatory penalties**. Any
  mismanagement or incorrect handling of sensitive
  data could lead to significant regulatory fines and
  legal actions.

- **Reputation risk**. Errors in compliance could
  severely damage the institution's reputation,
  eroding customer trust and competitive standing.

The solution

Recognizing the critical importance of maintaining
compliance, the institution implemented a data catalog with
the following features:

- **Detailed metadata management**. The catalog
  allowed for robust metadata management, making
  it easier to annotate, tag, and categorize data
  according to sensitivity levels and usage
  requirements.

- **Data lineage tracking**. The system tracked the flow
  and transformation of data, ensuring complete
  visibility into data usage. This was vital in

maintaining compliance with stringent regulations like GDPR and CCPA.

- **Integration with compliance tools.** The catalog was integrated with existing compliance monitoring and reporting tools to create a seamless workflow.

- **Access control and security measures.** The solution implemented strong security measures to protect sensitive data, including role-based access controls, encryption, and regular audits.

The outcome

The implementation of the data catalog brought about significant benefits:

- **Simplified compliance process.** The catalog provided a clear overview of data locations, movement, usage, and transformation, making the process of regulatory compliance more transparent and manageable.

- **Reduced operational costs.** With enhanced data governance, the institution spent less time and resources on managing compliance, resulting in reduced operational costs.

- **Lower regulatory risks**. The institution saw a marked reduction in regulatory risks thanks to more accurate compliance tracking and reporting.

- **Improved trust**. The transparent and robust management of sensitive data boosted trust with customers and stakeholders, enhancing the institution's reputation.

Conclusion

The experience of this financial institution highlights the essential role of data management in ensuring regulatory compliance within the financial sector. By implementing a robust data catalog, the institution was not only able to navigate the complex regulatory environment but also achieve operational efficiencies and build trust.

This case demonstrates the potential of modern data management tools in transforming the way financial institutions approach compliance. It serves as an insightful guide for other organizations in the financial industry that are seeking to modernize their compliance strategies. Leveraging technology for compliance is no longer an option but a necessity in today's highly regulated and data-driven financial landscape.

Telecommunications company

In the highly competitive telecommunications industry, understanding customer behavior and preferences is vital to crafting effective marketing strategies. Telecommunications companies often manage vast amounts of customer data, but this information is frequently siloed across various departments and systems. This fragmentation can hinder the ability to derive comprehensive insights and can impede marketing efforts. The following case study of a multinational telecommunications company illustrates how innovative data management strategies can overcome these challenges and drive deeper customer insights.

The challenge

A leading multinational telecommunications company was focused on leveraging customer data to optimize its marketing strategies. The challenges it faced were complex:

- **Siloed customer data**. The company's customer data was fragmented across various departments, including sales, customer service, marketing, and others. This made it challenging to gather and analyze comprehensive customer information.

- **Data quality concerns**. The lack of centralized management led to inconsistencies and potential inaccuracies in the data, undermining the reliability of insights.

- **Inefficient marketing strategies**. Without a holistic view of the customer, the company struggled to tailor marketing campaigns effectively, leading to missed opportunities for engagement and retention.

The solution

Determined to overcome these challenges, the company implemented a data catalog with the following key features:

- **Centralized data management**. The catalog provided a centralized system where all customer data could be gathered, categorized, and indexed, breaking down silos and facilitating a unified view.

- **Improved data governance**. The catalog ensured robust data governance, with mechanisms for data lineage tracking and quality control, guaranteeing the reliability and accuracy of the customer data.

- **Integration with analytics tools**. The catalog was integrated with data analytics and ML platforms, allowing seamless access to data for predictive modeling and personalization.

The outcome

The implementation of the data catalog led to several transformative outcomes:

- **Deeper customer insights**. By consolidating data, the catalog facilitated more in-depth and accurate insights into customer behavior, preferences, and needs.

- **Enhanced marketing effectiveness**. The improved data governance and analytics capabilities allowed the company to refine its marketing strategies, personalizing campaigns and targeting customers more precisely.

- **Higher customer engagement and retention**. The optimized marketing strategies resonated with customers, leading to higher engagement, satisfaction, and retention rates.

Conclusion

The journey of this multinational telecommunications company underscores the essential role of data cataloging in driving customer insights. By recognizing the challenges of siloed and fragmented data and implementing a robust data catalog, the company was able to enhance its marketing strategies and strengthen customer relationships.

This case provides valuable insights for other organizations seeking to leverage data for customer-centric strategies. It emphasizes the critical importance of centralized data management, integration with analytics tools, and a focus on data quality. The success of this initiative demonstrates that data cataloging is not merely a technical solution but a strategic enabler of organizational value and competitive advantage.

In conclusion, we see diverse applications of data cataloging, demonstrating its versatility and critical role in contemporary data management strategies. By examining these cases, organizations can draw lessons on the implementation, management, and optimization of data catalogs to drive organizational value. Whether in retail, healthcare, finance, or telecommunications, the thoughtful application of data cataloging can transform challenges into opportunities for growth and success.

Global petroleum company

A leading global petroleum company with operations spanning exploration, production, refining, distribution, and marketing faced challenges in managing the enormous volume and variety of data generated across its value chain. The complexity of the petroleum industry, coupled with stringent regulations and volatile market conditions, demanded a sophisticated approach to data management.

The challenge

Complex Data Landscape: The company dealt with a wide range of data, including geological surveys, production statistics, supply chain information, financial reports, and regulatory compliance documents:

- **Inefficient exploration efforts**. Lack of access to consolidated and accurate geological and seismic data hindered the efficiency of exploration activities.

- **Supply chain bottlenecks**. Disconnected data across different stages of the supply chain led to delays and inefficiencies, impacting profitability.

- **Regulatory compliance risks**. Managing compliance with environmental and safety regulations across different jurisdictions was challenging without a unified view of relevant data.

- **Security concerns**. Ensuring the security of sensitive data related to proprietary technologies, market strategies, and commercial agreements was a primary concern.

The solution

To overcome these challenges, the petroleum company implemented a robust data cataloging solution tailored to the specific needs of the oil and gas industry. The solution included:

- **Unified data repository**. Integrating data from various sources into a single catalog, providing a comprehensive view of the organization's operations.

- **Geospatial and seismic data integration**. A specialized module to manage and analyze geological and seismic data, enhancing exploration efforts.

- **Real-time supply chain analytics**. Connecting the data catalog with supply chain management tools to enable real-time tracking and optimization.

- **Compliance management system**. Implementing a system to monitor and ensure compliance with various regulatory requirements, including environmental and safety standards.

- **Advanced security protocols**. Employing state-of-the-art encryption and access control measures to safeguard critical business information.

The outcome

The implementation of the data cataloging solution led to transformative results for the petroleum company:

- **Optimized exploration activities.** Access to integrated geological data enabled more accurate predictions and decisions, leading to successful exploration efforts and reduced costs.

- **Streamlined supply chain.** Real-time insights into supply chain operations allowed for quick adjustments and optimization, minimizing delays and maximizing efficiency.

- **Compliance assurance.** Automated compliance tracking reduces the risk of violations, protecting the company from legal penalties and reputational damage.

- **Enhanced security.** Robust security measures ensure the integrity and confidentiality of critical business information.

- **Strategic decision-making.** The unified view of the company's operations facilitated data-driven decision-making, enabling the company to respond effectively to market trends and competitive pressures.

The conclusion

The case study of the global petroleum company illustrates the essential role that data cataloging can play in the complex and highly regulated environment of the oil and gas industry. By implementing a comprehensive data cataloging solution, the company was able to transform raw data into actionable insights, driving efficiency, compliance, and strategic growth.

This experience underscores the importance of a tailored approach to data management, recognizing the unique challenges and opportunities of the industry. It also highlights how technological innovation, when aligned with business objectives, can become a powerful enabler of success in an industry known for its complexity and volatility.

In a world where data is often referred to as the "new oil," this petroleum company's journey exemplifies how effectively harnessing data can lead to tangible benefits and competitive advantages, not just in the oil and gas sector but across various industries. It serves as a valuable lesson for other organizations seeking to leverage their data assets in a strategic and responsible manner.

Logistics company

In the fast-paced world of logistics, the ability to manage and analyze vast amounts of data is crucial for operational efficiency, customer satisfaction, and competitive advantage. Logistics companies must handle a wide array of information, including shipment tracking, inventory management, supplier data, and customer preferences. However, the fragmented nature of this data across various systems and platforms can lead to inefficiencies, inaccuracies, and missed opportunities. The following case study of a leading logistics company explores how these challenges can be addressed through innovative data management techniques.

The challenge

A major logistics company faced significant challenges related to the management and utilization of its extensive data landscape. The challenges included:

- **Disparate data sources**. Information related to shipments, inventory, suppliers, and customers were scattered across different systems, leading to a lack of coherence and visibility.

- **Operational inefficiencies**. The inability to access real-time, consolidated data hindered operational planning and execution, resulting in delays and inefficiencies in shipping, warehousing, and distribution.

- **Customer satisfaction issues**. Inaccurate or delayed data affected the company's ability to provide timely updates and personalized services to customers, impacting satisfaction and loyalty.

The solution

To tackle these challenges, the logistics company implemented a comprehensive data catalog with the following features:

- **Centralized data integration**. The catalog served as a hub where all relevant data could be gathered, indexed, and managed, providing a unified view of the logistics operations.

- **Data lineage and quality control**. The solution enabled tracking of data lineage and implemented quality checks to ensure the accuracy and reliability of information.

- **Real-time analytics integration**. The catalog was integrated with real-time analytics tools to facilitate dynamic decision-making and optimization of routes, inventory levels, and resource allocation.

- **Customer interface enhancement**. The system was connected to customer-facing platforms, allowing for personalized notifications, tracking, and support.

The outcome

The successful implementation of the data catalog led to transformative results:

- **Streamlined operations**. The integrated view of data enabled more efficient planning and execution across the entire logistics chain, from supplier management to final delivery.

- **Improved customer experience**. Enhanced data accuracy and real-time insights allowed for better customer communication and personalized services, leading to higher satisfaction and retention.

- **Cost savings**. By optimizing routes, inventory levels, and resource allocation, the company achieved significant cost savings and increased profitability.

- **Strategic insights and innovation**. The consolidated data facilitated advanced analytics,

328 • Data Cataloging

uncovering insights that drove strategic decision-making and innovation in services.

Conclusion

The case of this logistics company highlights the transformative power of integrated data management in the logistics industry. By recognizing the challenges of disparate data sources and implementing a robust data catalog, the company not only streamlined its operations but also enhanced customer satisfaction and achieved cost efficiencies.

This case serves as a valuable guide for other logistics organizations facing similar challenges. It illustrates the importance of centralized data management, real-time analytics integration, and a strong focus on data quality. The success of this initiative emphasizes that data cataloging is not just a tool for managing information but a strategic asset that can drive operational excellence, customer engagement, and business growth in the complex and competitive world of logistics.

Glossary

AI (Artificial Intelligence): Please see "Artificial Intelligence (AI)."

AWS Glue Data Catalog: A fully managed, scalable metadata catalog service provided by Amazon Web Services. It serves as a centralized repository for storing metadata about databases and tables.

Access Control: The selective restriction of access to data, typically involving authentication (verifying who you are) and authorization (determining what you can do).

Administrative Metadata: This type of metadata supports the management, use, and preservation of data. It includes rights management metadata, preservation metadata, and technical metadata.

Alation: A data cataloging platform that helps organizations create a single source of reference for all their data. Alation uses ML algorithms to inventory and document data assets across an organization automatically.

Alex Augmented Data Catalog: A data catalog tool that uses ML to automate the data inventory process and create a catalog of data assets.

Amazon Kinesis: An Amazon Web Services (AWS) platform that allows you to process large streams of data records in real-time.

Amundsen: An open-source data catalog project from Lyft. It aims to improve the productivity of data analysts, data scientists, and engineers when interacting with data.

Anomalies: In the context of data, anomalies refer to points in the data that are significantly different from others.

Anonymization and Pseudonymization: Techniques used to protect personal data by making it impossible (or significantly difficult) to connect data back to the individual it pertains to.

Apache Atlas: A scalable and extensible set of core foundational governance services by Apache that enables enterprises to effectively and efficiently meet their compliance requirements within Hadoop.

Apache Kafka: An open-source platform developed by the Apache Software Foundation, designed to handle real-time data feeds with high throughput and low latency.

Artificial Intelligence (AI): A branch of computer science that aims to create systems capable of performing tasks that usually require human intelligence. These tasks include learning from experience, understanding natural language, recognizing patterns, and making decisions.

Ataccama Data Catalog: Part of Ataccama ONE, this data catalog tool allows organizations to discover and understand their data landscape.

Audit Logging: The process of recording summary information about transactions for the purpose of audit compliance, security review, and operational analysis.

Automated Metadata Harvesting: The process of collecting metadata from various data sources in an automated manner and integrating it into the data catalog.

Azure Purview: A unified data governance service from Microsoft Azure that helps organizations achieve a holistic understanding of their data.

Batch Processes: A method of processing high volumes of data where a group (or batch) of data is collected over a period and then processed together.

Best Practices: A method or technique that has been generally accepted as superior to any alternatives because it produces results that are superior to those achieved by other means.

Big Data: Refers to datasets whose size, speed, or variety exceeds the ability of typical database software tools to capture, manage, and process within an acceptable timeframe.

Blockchain: A type of distributed ledger that stores a list of records, called blocks, which are linked using cryptography. Each block contains a cryptographic hash of the previous block, a timestamp, and transaction data. It is inherently resistant to modification of the data and brings an added layer of security and transparency.

Boomi Data Catalog and Preparation: A cloud-based, self-service data catalog and preparation tool from Boomi that provides visibility and control over data.

Business Glossary: A business glossary is a centralized reference tool that defines and standardizes key terms and concepts used within an organization, fostering clear communication, improved data management, and enhanced decision-making.

Business Intelligence (BI): Business intelligence refers to technologies, applications, and practices for the collection, integration, analysis, and presentation of business information. The purpose of BI is to support better business decision-making.

Business Intelligence (BI) Tools: Software that's used to analyze business data to help companies make decisions.

Business Metadata: Metadata that provides context about the data, such as business definitions, data ownership, and data stewardship.

CCPA (California Consumer Privacy Act): A state statute intended to enhance privacy rights and consumer protection for residents of California.

CKAN (Comprehensive Knowledge Archive Network): An open-source data portal platform that provides an out-of-the-box solution for managing, transferring, and accessing data.

Catalog: A systematic list, typically hierarchical, of data assets that include information such as data definitions, relationships, and metadata. It serves as a central reference for understanding and accessing data within an organization.

Collaboration Tools: Tools that facilitate the sharing of information and collaboration among users.

Collibra Catalog: A data cataloging tool that helps organizations find, understand, and trust their data. It's part of Collibra's data intelligence platform.

Crawling: In the context of data, it is a process of systematically scanning data sources to extract valuable metadata from those sources.

Data Analytics: Data analytics is the science of analyzing raw data in order to make conclusions about that information. It involves applying an algorithmic or mechanical process to derive insights and includes various techniques and processes.

Data Anonymization: The process of removing personally identifiable information from data sets so that the individuals whom the data describes remain anonymous.

Data Asset: Any data that is valuable for an organization. This could be customer data, financial data, or any other type of information that the organization uses in its operations or decision-making processes.

Data Catalog Engine: The heart of a data catalog that processes and organizes metadata stored in the metadata database, building a structured and searchable catalog.

Data Cataloging: The process of creating a collection of metadata, which includes information such as data origin, quality, lineage, and usage. It involves the management and organization of data to make it easily discoverable, accessible, and usable.

Data Cataloging Architecture: The holistic model that defines how different components related to data cataloging are organized, interacted, and performed.

Data Cataloging Layer: This layer houses the actual data catalog, which organizes and catalogs the ingested data.

334 • Data Cataloging

Data Classification: The process of organizing data by relevant categories so that it may be used and protected more efficiently.

Data Compliance: Refers to the act of adhering to, and demonstrating adherence to, a set of rules or requests established by governments and industry organizations that have regulatory authority over the topic.

Data Consumers: Any individual or entity that utilizes data in an organization, including data scientists, business analysts, data engineers, and decision-makers.

Data Democratization: The process by which data is made accessible to non-technical users within an organization, breaking down data silos and enabling a more inclusive data culture.

Data Dictionary: A collection of descriptions of data objects or items in a data model for the benefit of programmers and others who need to refer to them.

Data Discovery: This refers to the process of finding and understanding patterns and trends in data. The term emphasizes the explorative aspects of data analysis and is often associated with BI and data mining.

Data Distribution: A list that shows all possible values (or intervals) of the data and how often they occur.

Data Encryption: The method of using an algorithm to transform data into a form that is unreadable to unauthorized users.

Data Format: The way that data is stored or encoded. Data formats determine how data is interpreted and used by software programs.

Data Governance: The overall management of data availability, usability, integrity, and security in an organization. It includes a set of processes and a governance structure to ensure that critical data assets are formally managed throughout the enterprise.

Data Governance Tools: Software tools that can automate many data governance tasks and ensure consistent application of policies.

Data Ingestion: The process of importing, transferring, loading, and processing data for immediate use or storage in a database. It can include the ingestion of metadata, which describes the data's structure, content, and context.

Data Ingestion Layer: This layer is responsible for fetching the data from different sources, cleaning and pre-processing it, and ensuring its availability for further cataloging.

Data Integration: The process of combining data from different sources and providing users with a unified view of the combined data.

Data Integrity: The accuracy, consistency, and reliability of data.

Data Lake: A storage repository that holds a vast amount of raw data in its native format until it is needed.

Data Landscape: The various data sources, repositories, and databases within an organization, including both structured and unstructured data.

Data Lifecycle: The data lifecycle is the sequence of stages that a particular unit of data goes through, from its initial generation or capture to its eventual archival and/or deletion at the end of its useful life.

Data Lifecycle Management: The process of managing the flow of data throughout its lifecycle, from creation and initial storage to the time when it becomes obsolete and is deleted.

Data Lineage: The history of data, including where it originates from, where it moves over time, and what happens to it. It is a crucial aspect of data provenance and helps in understanding and verifying the state of the data.

Data Lineage Visualizer: A tool that provides a visual representation of where data comes from, how it moves, and how it changes over time.

Data Literacy: The ability to read, work with, analyze, and argue with data. It's a critical skill in a data-centric culture.

Data Management: The process of ingesting, storing, organizing, and maintaining the data created and collected by an organization. It helps in ensuring the accuracy and reliability of data.

Data Masking: A method of creating a structurally similar but inauthentic version of an organization's data that can be used for purposes such as software testing and user training.

Data Model: An abstract model that organizes elements of data and standardizes how they relate to one another and to properties of the real world.

Data Owners: The people responsible for the accuracy, quality, and integrity of a specific subset of data.

Data Privacy: Data privacy, also called information privacy, is the aspect of information technology that deals with the ability of an organization or individual to determine what data in a computer system can be shared with third parties.

Data Privacy Regulations: Legal rules and regulations that govern the collection, use, and storage of personal data, such as GDPR and CCPA.

Data Profiling: The process of examining, collecting statistics, and providing informative summaries about a data set to understand its quality and condition.

Data Profiling Reports: Documents that provide statistical analysis and assessment of data quality, consistency, and accuracy.

Data Provenance: This involves tracing the origin, ownership, and transformation history of data. It is like the data's "metadata fingerprint." It's crucial for understanding the sources of data, the transformations it has undergone, and the quality of its current state.

Data Quality: Data quality refers to the condition of a set of values of qualitative or quantitative variables. Good data quality corresponds to a high degree of data completeness, consistency, timeliness, accuracy, and relevance.

Data Quality Control: The process of ensuring that the data meets the specified quality criteria. It includes activities such as data cleansing, data integration, and data transformation.

Data Quality Metrics: Metrics that offer insights into the quality and reliability of the data.

Data Regulations: These are laws and guidelines that dictate what data can be collected and how it must be handled, with an emphasis on protecting the privacy of individuals included in the data.

Data Schema: An abstract representation of an organization's informational needs, including entities, attributes, and relationships.

Data Security: Protective digital privacy measures that are applied to prevent unauthorized access to computers, databases, and websites.

Data Security Policies: Guidelines put forth by an organization or industry to manage and protect information.

Data Source: The origin of data. It can include databases, data warehouses, data lakes, APIs, etc. Each data source has a unique metadata structure.

Data Source Layer: This includes all the different sources from where data is generated or gathered, such as databases, data warehouses, file systems, APIs, and other data storage units.

Data Standardization: The process of modifying data to fit a standard format, facilitating data integration, and ensuring uniformity across diverse datasets.

Data Standards and Procedures: Guidelines and processes are established to ensure consistent handling of data across an organization.

Data Stewards: Individuals responsible for data quality, data privacy, and data protection in an organization.

Data Stewardship: The management and oversight of an organization's data assets to help provide business users with high-quality data that is easily accessible in a consistent manner.

Data Transformation: The process of converting data from one format or structure into another format or structure.

Data Usage Analysis: The process of analyzing how data is used within an organization to identify critical datasets and how to prioritize their cataloging.

Data View: A representation of the data that allows users to interact with it and perform analysis without actually handling the raw data.

Data Warehouse: A large store of data accumulated from a wide range of sources within a company and used to guide management decisions.

Data-Driven Culture: A data-driven culture refers to an organizational culture that emphasizes decision-making based on data rather than intuition or observation alone.

Data.world: A cloud-based data cataloging platform that aims to break down silos and make data more accessible across organizations.

DataHub: A general-purpose metadata system developed by LinkedIn. It's designed for modern metadata scenarios, providing a unified view of a company's datasets, ML models, metrics, etc.

Database: A structured set of data stored in a computer, especially one that is accessible in various ways.

Dataset: A collection of data, usually presented in tabular form, where each column represents a particular variable, and each row corresponds to a given record.

Decentralization: Refers to the design principle where no single node or authority has control over the entire network. In blockchain, it ensures that no single party has complete control over the entirety of the data.

Decentralized Data Catalogs: Data catalogs that are not managed centrally. This might involve individual departments or users maintaining and managing their own data catalogs.

Denormalization: The process of combining tables to improve read performance, albeit at the cost of some data redundancy.

Dependencies: The relationships between tables are based on the interactions of the data items within the tables.

Descriptive Metadata: This type of metadata helps in finding and working with specific instances of data. It could include free-form text, controlled vocabularies, or unique identifiers.

Domain Integrity: A type of data integrity that defines the valid set of values for a column using data types, unique constraints, check constraints, and NOT NULL constraints.

Entity-Relationship Modeling : A type of database modeling that visually represents the system's entities, their attributes, and the relationships between them.

Erwin Data Catalog: A data cataloging solution that automates enterprise metadata management, data mapping, code generation, and data lineage.

Foreign Keys: Fields in a database table that link records in different tables, enabling data relationships.

GDPR (General Data Protection Regulation): A regulation in EU law on data protection and privacy in the European Union and the European Economic Area. It also addresses the transfer of personal data outside these areas.

Google Cloud Data Catalog: A fully managed and scalable data catalog service from Google Cloud designed to help organizations understand, discover, and manage their data.

Governance Frameworks: Structures that outline the processes, rules, and procedures used to ensure an organization's compliance with regulatory standards, laws, and internal policies.

HIPAA (Health Insurance Portability and Accountability Act): A federal law that required the creation of national standards to protect sensitive patient health information from being disclosed without the patient's consent or knowledge.

IBM Watson Knowledge Catalog: An enterprise data catalog from IBM that enables users to discover, catalog, and govern data across their organizations. It's part of IBM's suite of business analytics tools.

Immutability: In the context of blockchain, this refers to the quality that once data has been written to a blockchain, it cannot be changed. This ensures the permanence of the data and trust in its provenance.

Indexing: The process of creating an index for data to enable faster search and retrieval. Indexing structures data in a way that improves the speed of data query operations.

Informatica Enterprise Data Catalog: An AI-powered data catalog that provides a machine-learning-based discovery engine to catalog and classify data across the enterprise.

Interoperability: The ability of different systems, networks, and applications to work together and exchange information. In the context of data cataloging, blockchain could enhance interoperability by ensuring that data and metadata are consistently formatted and standardized across different systems.

IoT (Internet of Things): The network of physical objects embedded with sensors, software, and other technologies for the purpose of connecting and exchanging data with other devices and systems over the Internet.

K-Anonymity: K-Anonymity is a data anonymization technique that ensures that individual information in a dataset is indistinguishable from at least $k-1$ other individuals. By grouping data so that at least k individuals share any combination of quasi-identifiers, it protects privacy by preventing the re-identification of individuals within the dataset.

Legacy Systems: Old technology, computer systems, or applications that continue to be used, typically because the data or processes they handle cannot be easily moved to newer systems.

Lumada Data Catalog: A data cataloging tool from Hitachi Vantara that helps companies manage their data assets and comply with governance policies.

ML (Machine Learning): Please see "Machine Learning (ML)."

Machine Learning (ML): An application of AI that provides systems the ability to learn and improve from experience without being explicitly programmed automatically.

Magda: An open-source data catalog system developed by the Australian Government's Digital Transformation Agency. It's designed to be modular and easy to customize to suit different organizational requirements.

Maintenance Practices: The regular activities, methods, and procedures to keep a data catalog effective and reliable. This includes updates, error checking, and other tasks to ensure optimal operation.

Metacat: A unified metadata exploration API of distributed compute systems developed by Netflix. It allows a user to access system metadata in these distributed compute systems.

Metadata: Data that provides information about other data. In other words, it's data about data. Metadata can describe various aspects of a data item, such as its name, size, data type, etc. It aids in the organization, discovery, and management of data.

Metadata Database: The database where all extracted metadata is stored.

Metadata Extractors: Tools responsible for connecting to data sources, identifying relevant data, and extracting metadata from them.

Metadata Harvesting: The process of collecting metadata from various data sources. It is a critical step in populating a data catalog.

Metadata Management: The management of data that describes other data, known as metadata. It involves establishing policies and processes to ensure information can be integrated, accessed, shared, linked, analyzed, and maintained to the best effect across an organization.

Metadata Registry: A central repository for all metadata definitions. It should be easily accessible to stakeholders and should clearly document each metadata element, its meaning, usage instructions, and any other relevant information.

Missing Values: The absence of data or a data item in a data set.

Natural Language Processing (NLP): A field of AI that focuses on the interaction between computers and humans through natural language [Natural Language Querying (NLQ)]. The goal is to enable computers to understand, interpret, and generate human language in a valuable way.

Natural Language Querying (NLQ): A type of search that allows users to ask questions in natural, everyday language rather than using complex query languages.

Normalization: A method of organizing a database into tables and columns to minimize data redundancy and improve data integrity.

Operational Metadata: Metadata that provides operational details about the data, such as data quality scores and data lineage.

Oracle Cloud Infrastructure Data Catalog: A fully managed service that helps organizations discover, organize, enrich, and trace their data on Oracle Cloud.

Outliers: In statistics, an outlier is an observation that lies an abnormal distance from other values in a random sample from a population.

OvalEdge: A data catalog tool that aims to provide a comprehensive view of an organization's data, making it searchable, understandable, and governable.

Performance: In the context of data cataloging, performance refers to the efficiency and speed of operations related to data retrieval, processing, and management.

Performance Monitoring: The process of monitoring and measuring the performance of a system to provide the best user experience possible.

Policy Enforcement: The process of ensuring that all data handling practices comply with the organization's data governance policies.

Primary Keys: Unique identifiers for each record in a database table.

Privacy Regulations: Legal requirements that govern how organizations should protect personal data.

Proof of Concept (PoC): A demonstration, the purpose of which is to verify that certain concepts or theories have the potential for real-world application.

Qlik Catalog: A data cataloging tool from Qlik that delivers a user-friendly, self-service experience while ensuring data quality, accuracy, and governance.

Quantum Computing: A type of computation that leverages the principles of quantum mechanics. It's an area of study focused on the development of computer technologies centered around the principles of quantum theory.

Quasi-Identifiers: Quasi-identifiers are attributes in a dataset that, although not directly identifying, can be combined with other data to potentially reveal an individual's identity. They are key considerations in privacy techniques like *k-anonymity* to prevent re-identification.

Real-time Data Cataloging: The immediate cataloging and indexing of data as it streams into the data infrastructure.

Recommendations: (in the context of data cataloging) Suggestions made by a data cataloging system to assist users in finding relevant data or insights. These recommendations are typically powered by AI algorithms that analyze usage patterns and user queries.

Referential Integrity: A type of data integrity that ensures relationships between tables remain valid, typically enforced using foreign keys.

Regulatory Compliance: Adherence to laws, regulations, guidelines, and specifications relevant to an organization's business processes.

Regulatory Requirements: A set of principles, guidelines, or laws enforced by governing bodies that organizations must adhere to.

Relationship Inference: The process of identifying relationships between different data entities based on their usage, common attributes, and other clues.

Sandbox Environment: An isolated computing environment where data consumers can freely explore and manipulate data without affecting the original data sets or other users.

Scalability: The ability of a system, process, or a network to handle a growing amount of work or its potential to be enlarged to accommodate that growth.

Schema: The organization of data as a blueprint of how the database is constructed, encompassing information about data types, field descriptions, and relationships with other datasets.

Search Functionality: (in the context of data cataloging) Refers to the ability of a data cataloging system to locate data or insights based on a user's query. Practical search functionality enables quick and efficient data discovery.

Security and Governance Layer: This layer governs access controls, permissions, and privacy constraints.

Semantic Discovery: The process of identifying the meaning of data entities and attributes based on their names, descriptions, and contexts.

Semantic Search: Search with meaning, as distinguished from lexical search, where the search engine looks for literal matches of the query words or variants of them.

Single Source of Truth: A concept in information management that provides one view of data that everyone agrees on. It helps in maintaining consistency and accuracy of data across an organization.

Streaming Data: Data that is generated continuously by various sources and can be ingested in real or near-real-time.

Structural Metadata: This type of metadata emphasizes the container of the data, the interrelation of data entities, and their order.

Tableau Catalog: A feature of Tableau that provides visibility and understanding of the data used across the organization, supporting data discovery and governance.

Tagging: The process of assigning metadata to datasets, serving as a means to describe, categorize, and identify data.

Tags/Labels: Keywords associated with datasets to enhance their searchability. They could indicate the dataset's content, intended use case, or other categorical information.

Taxonomy Design: The process of classifying data into specific, defined categories based on certain characteristics or features, often represented by tags.

Tech Stack: The combination of programming languages, frameworks, and tools that developers use to build a web or mobile app.

Technical Metadata: Metadata that provides information about the data and the systems that create and manage it, including structure, tables, columns, data types, and more.

Transparency: In the context of blockchain, transparency refers to the ability of all participants in the network to see and verify the history of transactions. This enhances trust and verifiability in the data.

Uniqueness: A rule applied to ensure all data entries are unique and there is no duplication of data entries.

Usability: How easy an interface is to use.

Usage Metrics: Parameters that highlight how frequently a dataset is used and by whom.

User Interface (UI): The front end through which users interact with the catalog.

User Interface Layer: It provides an interface for users to access, explore, and manage the data catalog.

Value Ranges: The limits within which a data element can validly contain data.

Resources

Related Books

1. "The DAMA Guide to the Data Management Body of Knowledge, 2nd Edition (DAMA-DMBOK2)" by DAMA International
2. "Big Data, Big Dupe: A little book about a big bunch of nonsense" by Stephen Few
3. "Data Classification: Algorithms and Applications" edited by Charu C. Aggarwal
4. "The Data Warehouse Toolkit: The Definitive Guide to Dimensional Modeling" by Ralph Kimball and Margy Ross

Academic Journals and Papers

1. Journal of Big Data
2. International Journal of Data Science and Analysis
3. Data Science Journal
4. Journal of Data and Information Quality
5. Journal of Intelligent Information Systems
6. International Journal of Information Management
7. The Information Society: An International Journal
8. International Journal of Database Management Systems

Related Websites

1. DB-Engines Ranking – https://db-engines.com/en/
2. Towards Data Science – https://towardsdatascience.com/

3. Data Catalog Community –
   https://community.data.world/

4. Google's Dataset Search –
   https://datasetsearch.research.google.com/

5. Data Governance Institute –
   http://www.datagovernance.com/

6. Data Science Central –
   https://www.datasciencecentral.com/

7. KDNuggets – https://www.kdnuggets.com/

8. Data World – https://data.world/

Online Courses and Tutorials

1. Data Catalog Fundamentals – Udemy –
   https://www.udemy.com/topic/data-science/

2. Informatica Data Catalog Course – Coursera –
   https://www.coursera.org/informatica-data-catalog

3. Cataloging and Managing Data with AWS Glue –
   Pluralsight – https://www.pluralsight.com/courses/aws-
   big-data-glue-catalog-manage

4. Managing Big Data with MySQL – Coursera –
   https://www.coursera.org/learn/analytics-mysql

5. IBM Data Catalog Overview – Coursera –
   https://www.coursera.org/learn/ibm-data-catalog

6. Data Management and Visualization – Coursera –
   https://www.coursera.org/learn/data-visualization

Data Cataloging Tools

1. Alex Augmented Data Catalog – An AI-powered data
   catalog providing automatic data discovery. Website:
   https://alex.solutions/

2. Alation – A data cataloging tool that combines ML and human collaboration. Website: https://www.alation.com/

3. Amundsen – An open-source data catalog inspired by Lyft. Website: https://www.amundsen.io/amundsen/

4. Apache Atlas – An open-source data governance and metadata framework for Hadoop. Website: https://atlas.apache.org/

5. Ataccama Data Catalog – A cataloging tool that automatically discovers, profiles, and documents your data. Website: https://www.ataccama.com/product/data-catalog

6. AWS Glue Data Catalog – A central metadata repository, part of AWS Glue. Website: https://aws.amazon.com/glue/

7. Azure Purview – A unified data governance service that helps you manage and catalog data. Website: https://azure.microsoft.com/en-us/services/purview/

8. Boomi Data Catalog and Preparation – A tool that provides an interface to easily catalog, prepare, and deliver data. Website: https://boomi.com/platform/data-catalog-and-prep/

9. CKAN – An open-source data portal platform providing an out-of-the-box solution for managing, transferring, and accessing data. Website: https://ckan.org/

10. Collibra Catalog – A single, centralized data catalog to access and rationalize business and technical metadata. Website: https://www.collibra.com/data-catalog

11. Data.world – A cloud-native data catalog to map your siloed, distributed data to familiar and consistent business concepts. Website: https://data.world/

12. DataHub – An open-source metadata platform for the modern data stack. Website: https://datahubproject.io/

13. Erwin Data Catalog – A tool for automatically harvesting, transforming, and feeding metadata from a vast array of data sources, operational processes, business applications, and data models. Website: https://erwin.com/products/data-catalog/

14. Google Cloud Data Catalog – A fully managed and highly scalable data discovery and metadata management service. Website: https://cloud.google.com/data-catalog

15. IBM Watson Knowledge Catalog – An open and intelligent data catalog for managing enterprise data governance. Website: https://www.ibm.com/products/watson-knowledge-catalog

16. Informatica Enterprise Data Catalog – A tool that provides a machine-learning-based discovery engine to collect data across the enterprise while measuring data value. Website: https://www.informatica.com/products/data-catalog.html

17. Lumada Data Catalog – A tool that accelerates insights by automating data discovery, profiling, quality, and governance. Website: https://www.hitachivantara.com/en-us/products/data-management-analytics/lumada-data-catalog.html

18. Magda – An open-source data catalog for making datasets discoverable and presentable. Website: https://magda.io/

19. Metacat – A unified metadata exploration API of distributed storage systems. Website: https://netflix.github.io/metacat/

20. Oracle Cloud Infrastructure Data Catalog – A metadata management service that helps data professionals, analysts, data scientists, and data stewards collaborate and derive value from their enterprise data assets. Website: https://www.oracle.com/data-catalog/

21. OvalEdge – An innovative data catalog that enables organizations to discover and catalog data assets across multiple data sources. Website: https://www.ovaledge.com/

22. Qlik Catalog – A tool that helps to create a secure, enterprise-scale catalog of all the data your organization has available for analytics. Website: https://www.qlik.com/us/products/qlik-catalog

23. Tableau Catalog – A data cataloging functionality built into the Tableau platform, allowing for tracking data lineage and understanding data usage across the organization. Website: https://www.tableau.com/products/catalog

Data Cataloging Standards

1. Dublin Core Metadata Initiative – https://www.dublincore.org/specifications/

2. ISO/IEC 11179 – https://www.iso.org/standard/50340.html – Information technology — Metadata registries (MDR)

3. Data Catalog Vocabulary (DCAT) – https://www.w3.org/TR/vocab-dcat/ – W3C standard.

4. Metadata Encoding and Transmission Standard (METS)
    – https://www.loc.gov/standards/mets/
5. PREMIS (Preservation Metadata: Implementation
    Strategies) – http://www.loc.gov/standards/premis/

Professional Associations

1. DAMA International – https://www.dama.org/ – A non-
    profit, vendor-independent, global association of
    technical and business professionals dedicated to
    advancing the concepts and practices of information and
    data management.
2. Data Governance Professionals Organization –
    https://dgpo.org/ – A non-profit, vendor-neutral
    association of business, IT, and data professionals.

Index

www.ingramcontent.com/pod-product-compliance
Lightning Source LLC
Chambersburg PA
CBHW071539210326
41597CB00019B/3046